The
MONASTIC
RULES

The Augustine Series

Selected writings from "The Works of Saint Augustine—
A Translation for the 21st Century"

Volume IV

The Monastic Rules

Saint Augustine

The *MONASTIC* *RULES*

Foreword by
George Lawless, O.S.A.

Commentary by
Gerald Bonner

Translation and Notes by
Sister Agatha Mary, S.P.B.,
and Gerald Bonner

Edited by
Boniface Ramsey

New City Press
Hyde Park, New York

Published in the United States by New City Press
202 Cardinal Rd., Hyde Park, NY 12538
www.newcitypress.com

Cover design by Nick Cianfarani

Cover picture: Piero Strozzi: Depiction of Augustine, Doctor of the Church, wearing the black habit of the Augustinians (Biblioteca Medicea Laurenziana).

Library of Congress Cataloging-in-Publication Data:
A catalog record for this book is available from the Library of Congress

ISBN 1-56548-130-5

Printed in the United States of America

In Memory
of
Luc Verheijen, O.S.A.
indefatigable investigator
of
the monastic writings of
Augustine of Hippo

Contents

Foreword

As sinner and saint, talented theologian, penitent, polemicist, philosopher, and pastor of souls, Augustine of Hippo (modern Annaba in Algeria), is superbly well known. Appreciably less attention, however, has been directed towards Augustine as a monastic legislator and author. Consequently, it is a pleasure to preface this study of a highly elusive and complicated subject by a seasoned interpreter of the great North African Doctor of the Church. Another historian of early Christian thought correctly observes: "There are few literary problems so intricate as that of the documents which have been called 'Rules of St. Augustine.' "[1]

A seismic change in this area of research occurred during the middle decades of the twentieth century with the publication of Luc Verheijen's *La Règle de Saint Augustin*, I, *Tradition Manuscrite*; II, *Recherches Historiques* (Paris: Études Augustiniennes, 1967). These two volumes constitute a landmark in the history of Augustinian scholarship and fulfill "an important and exhaustive task," words which Augustine applied to himself in the *Preface* to his *City of God*. Although by no means perfect, Verheijen's unrelenting research established some permanent signposts for marking the ground and clearing the field in the otherwise intractable terrain of textual criticism. History will decide whether Verheijen has merely moved the goal posts or actually pushed the boundaries of our knowledge to their present limits.[2]

Five literary genres are represented in Augustine's ensemble of monastic writings: *libellus, libri, epistulae, sermones ad populum,* and *enarrationes in Psalmos* (this last Latin word coined by Erasmus in the sixteenth century as the title for Augustine's expositions of the Book of Psalms). We shall examine them in turn.

The Rule of Saint Augustine

The text identifies itself in its final paragraph as a *libellus,* "little book" (8. 2). Like Basil of Caesarea, its author seems never to have thought of it as a *regula*, or rule. The use of this word to describe a monastic genre, it should be noted, was a late arrival in western Latin vocabulary. In this instance, Eugippius of Lucullanum (now Pizzofalcone near Naples), was the first to label the document a *Rule* and to affix Augustine's name to it. We are not without complexities in this matter and in other areas also. Sufficient for our present purpose are the following observations: manuscripts identifying Augustine as author are plentiful prior to the twelfth century; verbatim citations, similarity of contents, uses of scripture, affinities, allusions from the *Rule* that bears his name are compellingly aligned with many uncontested works of Augustine; and the neologism, *emendatorius,* appears for the first time in the bishop's authentic writings and in the *Rule* (4, 9) attributed to him in the manuscript tradition.

The basic inspiration of the *Rule* derives from the Scriptures with heavy debts, however, to Luke-Acts and St. Paul. Such hermeneutical and doctrinal perspectives are by no means limited to the bishop's monastic writings. They extend to his entire oeuvre and are enunciated thus: "In the Scriptures we have learned to recognize Christ, in the Scriptures we have learned to recognize the Church" (Letter 105. 4.14).

One should recall that monasticism was a lay movement in the early Church. The *Rule* is a non-clerical document addressed to a single house. On the basis of internal evidence (there is no other), I am persuaded that its immediate addressees were the laymen frequently described in the text as "brothers" or "household servants of God," who lived in the garden monastery at Hippo established there by Augustine in 391. Unlike the *Rule* of Benedict,[3] there is no indication in the text that the document was designed for distribution to other houses.

Although a single text, there are two versions, masculine and feminine. In the succeeding generation Caesarius and Aurelian of Arles evidently felt the need to compose distinctive *Rules* for both sexes. In Augustine's case, the chief difference between the masculine and feminine versions is basically their grammatical gender and six interpolations which Verheijen's conservative textual criticism disallows. In her translation from the Latin Sister Agatha Mary has helpfully marked off with brackets *ad locum* these disputed passages. Scholars remain divided in their opinion as to which version takes precedence in time.

Unlike John Cassian of Marseilles who outlived Augustine by about five years, and unlike Benedict in the next generation, Augustine did not specify monastic attire in his *Rule*. The "inner clothing of the heart" (5.1) was more preferable than "clothes that attract attention" (4.1). Augustine's interiorism evidently had no special need of symbolic dress or of retreat into the desert. The bishop's desert also was largely a matter of the human heart, never a matter for geographical relocation.[4] His was an "urban monasticism" bearing witness in the public square or market place of this world. Augustine's use of *saeculum*, "the spirit of the age," four times instead of the spatial term, *mundus*, is presumably occasioned by the need for a word with temporal associations utterly devoid of Manichaean resonances, so as not to dilute the Judeo-Christian doctrine of creation.

Augustine's mindset reflects a culture that was both secular and sacred. His *Rule* took for granted the existence of a library where he had room for non-canonical Scriptures such as the Acts of John (*Homily on the Gospel of John* 124.2 and 7) and the Apocalypse of Paul (*ibid.* 98.8).[5] The fact that this first western monastic rule provided for a library reveals something about its author's expectations for members of his community. One is prompted to ask whether permission to visit the local baths for reason of ill health and personal hygiene could be granted for other reasons as well. The ancient baths also served as "leisure centers" for various cultural activities such as public declamation, poetry readings, lectures and physical exercises. Augustine's well-educated friend Firmus, married to a Christian, had been anything but firm in his resolution to petition baptism. Together they had visited the local baths for three consecutive afternoons in order to listen to a public reading of the eighteenth book of the bishop's *City of God* (Divjak, Letter 2*). Could it have been that options for learning and study available within the monastery became broadened to embrace extramural interests of a similar kind? It is unfortunate that a prescriptive document such as the *Rule* sometimes reads like brief bulletin-board notices, which require further explication, thereby falling short of telling us all that we would like to know.

His monastic *Rule* (3.5) blends an adage from the philosopher Lucius Annaeus Seneca (*Letter to Lucilius* 2.6) and Luke-Acts 4:35 to express the sharing of possessions and their distribution in community (*communis vita* I, 7). The *Rule* likewise echoes the counsel of Cicero's *Tusculan Disputations* 4. 9. 21 on the subject of anger and hatred (6.1).[6] An amalgam of Stoic political-ethical philosophy from Cicero is melded with 1 Cor 13: 5; 12: 31 and also Acts 4: 35 to monitor the interaction between the common good (*commune*) and the individual good (*proprium*) as a cardinal principle in Augustine's understanding of community life (5.2).[7]

Augustine prescribes the company of others, "no fewer than two or three" (5.7), when a brother or sister is required by the superior to visit the public baths for hygienic purposes, reasons of poor health, constipation, or simply to get warm in winter. This precept of companionship enables brothers with God's help to safeguard chastity by mutual concern for one another (4.6). There is no prohibition in the *Rule* against eye contact with women outside the monastery, except never to ogle or to stare at them (and vice versa in the feminine version, 4.4), as is customary in many countries bordering the Mediterranean Sea even today. In marked contrast, Cassian offers one of his many transplants from an eastern Egyptian monastic tradition to the western by citing an ancient saying from the Desert Fathers: "a monk must by all means flee from women and bishops" (*Inst.* 11.18). Like Cassian, Augustine appears to be seldom at ease in the company of women,[8] though he is far less parochial and puritanical in this matter.[9]

The same is true of their respective approaches to friendship. Whereas the classical tradition rooted in Pythagoras, Plato, Aristotle and Cicero enriched Augustine's understanding of friendship, Cassian's rather monochrome Sixteenth Conference *De amicitia* is limited to the Stoic ideal and could more suitably be entitled *De concordia in claustro.*[10] In the manner of bookends, nine instances of *amicitia* hold Cassian's Conference together.[11] Its titular theme, nonetheless, becomes submerged as somewhat secondary, with friendship functioning as the anodyne for the restraint and curative control of anger. Lacking entirely in Cassian are Augustine's many positive valuations of *amicitia* or those of Gregory Nazianzen, Paulinus of Nola and others.[12]

Three Treatises: Work, Marriage, Virginity

An early book, *The Way of Life of the Catholic Church,* as its title indicates, expresses Augustine's personal conviction that the phenomenon of monasticism is triangulated between Christ, Church and monastery. During the second decade of the fifth century Augustine referred to "the current vogue of virginity" (*nova virginitas,* Sermon 304.2). A generation earlier Ambrose had been an over-ardent exponent of virginity with four treatises on the subject.[13] The same can be said for Jerome, unfortunately, at the additional cost of disparaging marriage. Both Fathers of the Church were overreacting to the intransigent and anti-ascetic stance of the monk Jovinian who, although celibate himself, set no value on either virginity or asceticism. Augustine refreshingly revitalizes the debate with three treatises on work, the excellence of marriage, and holy virginity, in that order. The sequence of composition is noteworthy for the moderate ascetic exercises which punctuate each of these three books. It will be noted further that Augustine's sensible equilibrium tempers the excessive enthusiasm of Ambrose, while at the same time restraining the acerbic rigorism of Jerome and rejecting the erroneous views of Jovinian.

While the theme of manual labor was a *topos* in ancient Latin literature ever since the early Republican times of Cato the Censor's *De agricultura* (sometimes known as *De re rustica*), Augustine is the only Christian author, in either East or West, to be associated with a free-standing book-length format addressed to monks on the subject of work. Here the bishop parts company with Cassian and Benedict of Nursia, both of whom integrate domestic chores in the monastery (as Augustine himself does in his *Rule*) and manual labor in the orchards and fields into their respective writings. In his *Asceticon,* which eventually gave birth to the titles, *Longer* and *Shorter Rules*, Basil of Caesarea had anticipated Augustine, Cassian and Benedict in this manner of composition. Augustine, meanwhile, in a separate book, *The Work of Monks,* notes the perverse inconsistency of monks who refuse to work, while at the same time demanding leisure time for reading the very Scriptures that describe work not as something optional but inherently human, and enriched all the more by its conjunction with Christian faith. Augustinian irony is pressed into further service when the bishop asks whether such long-haired brothers wished to share their monastic leisure (*otium*) with the local barbers by denying them employment (*negotium*). Also, it is rather silly for monks to fancy themselves "eunuchs for the kingdom of God." Women too, the bishop reminds the monks, are made in the image of God.

Epistles

In like manner, Augustine offers a balance sheet on the respective merits of monastic leisure and apostolic activity in the life of the Church (Letter 48).[14] Their harmonization in the life of an individual becomes possible within a communitarian setting. The active and contemplative lives, argues Augustine, while at first blush seemingly antithetical to each other, need not become mutually antagonistic. Monastic life and clerical life, furthermore, reveal more dissimilarities than similarities. Augustine laments Aurelius' premature ordination of a monk named Donatus who had deserted the Hippo monastery. Donatus' situation was different from that of his brother, who had likewise left the monastery and was not yet ordained. For the Bishop of Carthage to ordain so unqualified a person to the priesthood was offensive to everyone concerned. Lay people are again interpreting the common saying: "A bad flute player makes a good singer in a choir" to mean instead: "A bad monk makes a good cleric" (Letter 60.1). Augustine pushes the issue a step further by noting that "at times even a good monk does not make a good cleric." The letter then alludes indirectly to the necessary preparation for priesthood and the perils of pastoral life.[15] The lines of demarcation between monk and cleric, however clearly defined in the bishop's mind, were to earn even greater precision in the sunset of his life from his contemporary Cassian of Marseilles and a generation later from Benedict of Nursia.

Letter 111 describes migratory people in Iberia, Italy, and Gaul, a foretaste of the Gothic and Vandal invasions, and also "the brigandage of the Donatist and Circumcellion clergy" in North Africa during the first third of the fifth century. Oddly enough, Isidore of Seville will identify the

Circumcellions as a fifth classification of monks.[16] Augustine's Letter 157.23-29 sheds light on the question of riches and poverty, emphatically parting from Pelagian perspectives as these are found in the anonymous treatise *De divitiis*, while offering a personal reflection on the scriptural verse, "Sell what you have and give to the poor" (Mt 19:21), which was one of his favorites (*vehementer adamavi*, Letter 157.39). Letter 210, translated in this volume, deals with the protocol of correction in a convent of nuns. In the problematic Letter 211, likewise partly translated here, the ruckus in the convent is described as a *seditio,* a civil war. Letter 243 reveals an incisive description of Augustinian characteristics in a monastic calling.[17]

Sermons to the People: the Life of Clerics

Sermons 355 and 356 are companion pieces, unabashedly autobiographical, detailing a breach of common life and defining in the bishop's words "the purpose" (*propositum*) and "the law governing our life together" (*lex vitae nostrae,* Sermon 355.2). That the bishop himself repeated verbatim the words from the Acts of the Apostles 4:31-35, after they had just been read aloud by the deacon, Lazarus, likewise accentuates this fact. These two sermons reveal the rule of life which inspired the men who were living in the "bishop's house" (*domus episcopi*) or the "monastery of clerics" (*monasterium clericorum,* Sermon 355.2). The garden monastery of 391, as we noted above, furnished the setting for non-clerical brothers who wished to live a "common life" (*communis vita,* 1.7). The only cleric in the garden monastery was the presbyter, or priest, who is mentioned four times. The distinction between "conscience" and "reputation" in the first paragraph of Sermon 355 indicates that the "monastery of clerics" was an apostolic community with pastoral outreach. In many ways the outcome of the proceedings in both sermons anticipates the truth of the matter in the wise observation of Pope Paul VI: "Modernity listens more willingly to witnesses, and if it does listen to teachers, it is because they are witnesses" (*Evangelii Nuntiandi* 41).

Expositions of the Psalms

Both individually and as members of Christ's body, all faithful Christians are recognized as the "temple of God" (1, 8; *Exposition of Psalm* 131). This precious Pauline insight (2 Cor 6:16) is by no means limited to the bishop's writings on monastic life. Elsewhere Augustine offers a vivid description of laity, clergy, monks, and nuns (*Exposition of Psalm* 99.8-13), thus radically repudiating the heretical errors of Manichaean asceticism (the elect and the hearers), Donatist separatism (saints and sinners), and Pelagian perfectionism (the elite and the non-elite).[18] Monasteries have their origin in the Church which, in turn, takes its origin from Christ. Five references to the Holy Spirit in *Exposition of Psalm* 132 reflect Augustine's pivotal teaching of *Christus totus,* the "whole Christ," in which the Spirit is identified as the source of love and holiness in Church, monastery, and home.

Augustine's admonition in Sermon 96.9, meanwhile, serves notice to his readers and listeners that "in this holy world" the following of Christ is incumbent upon everyone: virgins, married couples, widows and widowers, monks, clergy, and laity of every stripe. All have their place and are invited to follow the Lord in a lifestyle which is consonant with their respective states of life. Lastly, many admirable traits and features of Greco-Roman urbanity and sociability survived both the sack of Rome and the Vandal invasions of north Africa in the clearly discernible form of Christian humanism. As evidenced from this ensemble of monastic texts, Augustine's enrichment of that heritage in Western culture is far from negligible.

Five commentaries of differing length on Augustine's *Rule* are the product of European research: British (Sister Agatha Mary, 1992); Dutch (Tarcisius van Bavel, 1982, with these translations: English, 1984; Italian and Spanish, 1986; French, 1989; and German 1990); Italian (Agostino Trapé, 1986); French (Luc Verheijen, vol. 1, 1980; Italian trans., 1986; vol. 2, 1988; Italian trans., 1993); and German (Adolar Zumkeller, 1962; English trans., 1987).

The present volume is a worthy companion to all three and a most welcome addition. American and Canadian scholarship await their turn.

George Lawless, O.S.A.
Feast of the Conversion of St. Augustine
Rome, 24 April 2003

Notes

* All references are to the *Rule* (*Praeceptum*) unless noted otherwise.

1. Louis Boyer, *La spiritualité du Nouveau Testament et des Pères* (Paris: Editions Montaigne 1960; Eng. Tr., *The Spirituality of the New Testament and the Fathers*, Paris: Burns and Oates/Desclée, 1963) 495.

2. The rather summary dismissal of Luc Verheijen's research by Georges Folliet is unfair. See *"Le Monachisme en Afrique de Saint Augustin à Saint Fulgence,"* in *Il Monachesimo Occidentale dalle Origini alla Regula Magistri*. XXVI Incontro di studiosi dell'antichità cristiana. Rome 8-10 May 1997. Institutum Patristicum Augustinianum. *Studia Ephemeridis Augustinianum* 62 (Rome, 1998) 291-315 at 295-297.

3. See RB 18, 22; 62, 1 and 73, 1. Timothy Fry, OSB, ed., RB 1980. *The Rule of St. Benedict* (Collegeville, Minn.: Liturgical Press, 1981) 295, n. 73. 1.

4. George Lawless, "Eremus," *Augustinus-Lexikon,* (Basel: Schwabe & Co., 1996-2002), v. 2: 1086-1092.

5. Henry Chadwick, "Augustine" in *A Dictionary of Biblical Interpretation*. Eds., R. J. Coggins and J. L. Houlden (London: SCM Press, 1990) 65-69 at 67.

6. Luc Verheijen, "The Straw, the Beam, the *Tusculan Disputations* and the *Rule* of Saint Augustine: On a Surprising Augustinian Exegesis, *Augustinian Studies* 2 (1971) 17-36.

7. Cicero, *de officiis* 1. 20-22, 31, 51, 85, 3. 21-31, 52.

8. See chapter 26 of Possidius, *Life of Augustine;* also, Gerald Bonner, "Augustine's Attitude to Women and *Amicitia,"* in *Homo Spiritalis. Festgabe für Luc Verheijen, OSA zum 70. Geburstag*, ed., C. Mayer (Würzburg: Augustinus-Verlag, 1987) 259-275.

9. George Lawless, *"infirmior sexus . . . fortior affectus*: Augustine's Jo. ev. tr. 121, 1-3: Mary Magdalene," in *Augustinian Studies*, 34:1 (2003) 107-118. The bishop's mature appreciation of *femina* is recapitulated in his understanding of the first Easter morning. The encounter of Mary Magdalene with the Risen Jesus, whom she mistakes for a gardener, and Augustine's deft use of language to interpret the scene, show a determination on his part to supersede somewhat threadbare biblical and patristic prejudices against women, the bulk of which resulted from the confluence of convention and culture. The reactions of the Magdalene to the discovery of the empty tomb, when contrasted with those of the disciples and apostles, prompt Augustine to offer a positive view of women and a confi-

dent estimate of human emotions in the formation of personal faith in the Risen Jesus. Finally, the Eve-Mary, the mother of Jesus-Mary Magdalene trajectory confirms enduring feminine presence in the story of salvation and its importance, to say nothing of its fully shared status with men as images of God and possessors of permanent embodiment alongside the Risen Lord (*City of God* 22, 17).

10. Brian Patrick McGuire, *Friendship and Community. The Monastic Experience*. Cistercian Studies 95 (Kalamazoo: Cistercian Publications, 1988) 78-81, at 79.

11. David Konstan, "Problems in the History of Christian Friendship," *Journal of Early Christian Studies,* 41:1 (1996) 87-113 at 106.

12. *John Cassian: The Conferences,* translated and annotated by Boniface Ramsey, Ancient Christian Writers 57 (New York, NY: Paulist Press, 1997) 553.

13. Boniface Ramsey, *Ambrose* (London and New York: Routledge, 1997) 60-61.

14. Bernard Bruning, "*Otium* and *Negotium* Within the One Church, *Epistula* 48," *Augustiniana* 51 (2001) 104-149.

15. A viewpoint expressed ten years previously to his bishop Valerius: "Nothing in this life, and especially at this time, is more difficult, more laborious, and more dangerous than the office of bishop, priest, or deacon" (Letter 21, 1).

16. *Ecclesiastical Duties* 2, 16.

17. M. Fiedrowicz, "*Castra ne deseras* (*ep.* 243.1): Riflessioni agostiniane sull'abbandono della vita monastica," *Studia Ephemeridis Augustinianum* 62 (1998) 333-339.

18. George Lawless, "Augustine's Decentring of Asceticism," in *Augustine and His Critics. Essays in Honour of Gerald Bonner,* eds., Robert Dodaro and George Lawless (London and New York: Routledge, 2000) 142-163 at 145-148 and 152.

Background of Augustine's Rules

The four documents translated in this volume are commonly acknowledged by scholars to be associated with, though not necessarily written by, Augustine of Hippo. They are the fundamental material for determining his place as a monastic legislator in Western Christendom. In order to simplify subsequent discussion, they need to be listed and described at the outset. (The names by which they are called are those employed by Luc Verheijen.)

1. The *Ordo Monasterii,* known in the middle ages as the *Regula secunda* is a short document of less than 400 words, giving an outline of the monastic horarium, liturgical details of the daily office, and general directions regarding the behavior of the members of a masculine religious community.

2. The *Praeceptum* or *Regula tertia.* This is the *Rule* of Saint Augustine *par excellence* and is observed by contemporary followers of Augustine with minor additions. It is concerned with the life of a masculine community.

3. The *Obiurgatio* is Augustine's Letter 211, sections 1-4. It is a rebuke addressed to a community of nuns who have rebelled against their superior and appealed to Augustine to intervene in order to settle their dispute. In many manuscripts this rebuke commonly precedes

4. The *Regularis Informatio* or feminine version of the *Praeceptum.* Since the sixteenth century it has been widely considered that this is the original Augustinian *Rule*, offered by Augustine to a convent of quarreling nuns, and that the *Praeceptum* is an adaptation made in the twelfth century for the use of male communities. Recent scholarship, notably that of Luc Verheijen, has cast serious doubt on this position.

I

The Author of the Rules

This section seeks to present the reader who has no specialized knowledge of Augustinian monastic studies with the results of recent study, notably by Luc Verheijen.[1] It must be said at the outset that it is a difficult undertaking, given the complicated character of the research, which involved Verheijen in an exhaustive study of the manuscript tradition of the four source-documents and their combinations in various codices. It should, however, be emphasized that the conclusions drawn from this research, although persuasive, are not, and cannot be, absolutely compelling, since we lack any direct statement by Augustine that he ever composed a monastic rule.

Augustine of Hippo spent half his life as a monk. He wrote and preached on monastic life in community, required his episcopal household to live as monks,[2] and was regarded in the middle ages in Western Europe as a monastic legislator second only to Benedict of Nursia. During the twentieth century the four monastic documents which may reasonably be associated with him have been subjected to rigorous textual investigation, which has appeared convincing to most scholars who have studied the matter, but this has not led to unanimity regarding their origins. In this field the work of Luc Verheijen, and particularly his two-volume study, *La Règle de Saint Augustin*, has made an outstanding—some would say decisive—contribution. Verheijen's conclusions were made available to English readers by George Lawless, in his *Augustine of Hippo and his Monastic Rule*. However, traditional opinion was not easily shaken, and it was still possible, as late as 1983, for an article in a theological dictionary to deny the authenticity of any of the rules associated with Augustine's name.

An initial difficulty for the student is that while Augustine was undoubtedly influenced by monastic ideals and practices—his decision to seek baptism at Milan in 386 was initiated by learning of Saint Antony the first monk and his imitators in the desert,[3] and he was aware of the ejaculatory prayers commended by the monks of Egypt[4]—he nowhere claims to have composed a rule, nor is one listed in the *Indiculum*, the catalogue of his writings compiled by his friend and biographer Possidius of Calama. The first ascription to him of the two rules commonly associated with his name is by his admirer, Eugippius of Lucullanum, near Naples (c.465-c.539), the biographer of Saint Severinus of Noricum, who began the compilation of monastic rules which constituted his own rule with the complete texts of the *Ordo Monasterii* (*Ante omnia, fratres carissimi, diligatur deus, deinde proximus* . . .) followed by the *Praeceptum* (*Haec sunt quae ut observetis praecipimus* . . .), separated only by the word *Amen* and ending with the words: *Explicit Regula Sancti Augustini Episcopi.*[5] With these two rules, the *Ordo Monasterii* and the *Praeceptum*, there was associated in the early middle ages another, the *Regula Consensoria* or *Regula prima*, perhaps of seventh-century Spanish origin.[6] All these pieces appeared in the first edition of Augustine's works, published by John Amerbach at Basel in 1506. The authenticity of the *Regula prima* (text in Verheijen, II, 7-9) had, however, already been challenged in the fourteenth century by the Augustinian friar Jordan of Quedlinburg in Saxony, and was excluded by Erasmus from his edition of Augustine's works, published by Froeben in 1528. No one seems subsequently to have disputed Erasmus's judgment on this matter and the *Regula Consensoria* may for our purposes be removed from consideration.

Erasmus also questioned the Augustinian authorship of the *Regula secunda*—the *Ordo Monasterii*—and most recent scholars before Verheijen tended to agree with him in denying Augustinian authorship, with the notable exception of the Dominican, Pierre Mandonnet, while considering that the work probably had some connection with the Bishop of Hippo. So far as the *Regula tertia* was concerned, Erasmus accepted it as an authentic work of Augustine but suggested that it was a transcription into masculine form of his Letter 211, sections 5-16, addressed to a convent of nuns, where Augustine's sister had formerly been superior. Erasmus here proposed an hypothesis which was later endorsed by Cardinal Robert Bellarmine (1542-1621), became widely accepted, and still finds favor with distinguished scholars at the present day.[7]

We are left then with three monastic rules in some way associated with Augustine: the *Ordo Monasterii*, of which the earliest example is the copy in Eugippius' *Rule*, preserved in a manuscript of the sixth or seventh century, now in the Bibliothèque Nationale in Paris, MS Latinus 12634; the *Praeceptum*, which follows the *Ordo* in the same codex; and the feminine version of the *Praeceptum*, called the *Regularis Informatio*, which occurs in Augustine's *Letter* 211, sections 5-16, preceded by an opening passage (*Letter* 211, sections 1-4), called by Verheijen the *Obiurgatio,* in which Augustine rebuked the recipients for the disorders in their convent, which had led to a request to him to remove their superior from office. These two parts, the *Obiurgatio* and the *Regula Informatio*, are frequently copied in the manuscripts as a single whole. However, in the oldest complete text, the Codex Turicensis Rhenaugiensis (Zürich, MS Rheinau 89), of the late eleventh/early twelfth century, the two portions are separated by the words: *Explicit p[rae]facio. Incip[it] regula monialium a beato augustino edita*—"Here ends the preface. Here begins the rule for nuns composed by Blessed Augustine,"[8] while the oldest manuscript witness to *Letter* 211, the tenth-century Madrid MS Escorial a I 13 contains, in the words of Verheijen, "a fragment of the *Obiurgatio*, preceded by the debris of the address: *Augustinus in domino salutem. Amen,*" and followed by the words: "*Statui vobis praecepta vivendi scribere quae ut observetis praecipimus in monasterio constitutae* (I have decided to write to you the precepts which we advise you to observe, who are settled in a monastery)," taken from the *Regularis Informatio.*[9]

We have, therefore, four fundamental documents: the *Ordo Monasterii*; the *Praeceptum*; the *Regularis Informatio*, the feminine version of the *Praeceptum;* and the *Obiurgatio*, the rebuke to quarreling nuns. As might be expected, however, in the centuries of manuscript copying, longer combinations have emerged. In order to indicate the complexity of the textual transmission, these ought to be mentioned, though they do not in themselves affect the origin or resolve the attribution of the four basic documents.

The *Praeceptum Longius.* This is the *Ordo Monasterii* immediately followed by the *Praeceptum*. It is the form found in Eugippius.

The *Regula recepta*. This consists of the first sentence of the *Ordo Monasterii*: *Ante omnia, fratres carissimi, diligatur deus, deinde et proximus, quia ista sunt praecepta principaliter nobis data*—"Before all else, dearest brothers, let God be loved, and then your neighbor, because these are the chief commandments which have been given us"—followed by the *Praeceptum*. This is the form of the *Rule* used by contemporary followers of Augustine.[10]

The *Epistula Longior*. This is the *Obiurgatio* and the *Regularis Informatio* combined to form a single unit in Letter 211 printed by Goldbacher in the *Corpus Scriptorum Ecclesiasticorum Latinorum* 57, 356-371 and re-edited by Verheijen, I,49-66.[11]

The *Ordo Monasterii feminis datus*. This is the feminine version of the *Ordo Monasterii* , on which see Verheijen, I, 40-45, 140-145.

The *Epistula Longissima*. This is a combination of part of the *Obiurgatio* with the *Ordo Monasterii feminis datus* and passages of the *Regularis Informatio*.[12] See Verheijen, I, 176.

This catalogue of various combinations suggests the complexity of the manuscript material which Luc Verheijen traced, examined, and analyzed. Altogether he examined 274 codices containing 317 treatises[13] and accumulated more information than any previous worker in this field. This fact is important, because much of his argument was conditioned by his vast and unequaled knowledge of the source material, unfamilar to earlier scholars.

Let us now return to the relation of Augustine to the four monastic documents associated with his name. Augustine, it will be recalled, never declared that he had composed a monastic rule in the *Revisions*, the critical bibliography of his writings which he composed in 427, three years before

his death. This consideration against his possible authorship is not, however, as decisive as might appear. First, he
could have omitted it by oversight, as happened in the case
of his anti-Pelagian treatise, *De Perfectione Iustitiae Hominis*.
Secondly, and more important, the *Praeceptum*, the masculine version of the *Rule*, could have been composed for the
private use of Augustine's own community, in which case it
might have been deliberately excluded from the *Revisions*,
which lists compositions which, even when addressed to
individuals, were designed for a wider readership.

Furthermore, stylistic parallels can be found between the
Praeceptum and some of Augustine's other writings like the
De Opere Monachorum of 400, the *De Continentia*, of uncer-
tain date but perhaps from 418-420, and Letter 189, written
in 418.[14] Verheijen has suggested that a passage of
Possidius' *Life of Augustine,* 5.1—

> Once a priest it was not long before he established
> a monastery within the precincts of the church [at
> Hippo] and entered upon a life with the servants
> of God in accordance with the method and rule
> established under the holy apostles. Above all, no
> one in that community might have anything of his
> own, but they were *to hold everything in common* and
> it was to be *distributed to each one as he had need* (Acts
> 2:44-45; 4:35)[15]

—might be an echo of the *Praeceptum* 1.3—

> And then, you should not call *anything your own but
> you should have everything in common* (Acts 4:32).
> *Food and clothing* (1 Tm 6:8) should be allotted to
> you by your superior, not equally to all because
> you are not all equally strong, but to each one

according to need. For thus you read in the Acts of the Apostles: *They had everything in common and distribution was made to each as any had need* (Acts 4:32.35).

This combination of Acts 4:32b + 32c +35b, according to Verheijen, is to be found in patristic literature only in Possidius and in the *Praeceptum.*[16]

Clearly, this particular piece of evidence does not establish Augustine as the author of the *Praeceptum.* It could equally apply to the *Regularis Informatio,* where the wording is the same, except that *praeposita* (prioress) is substituted for the *praepositus*(superior) of the *Praeceptum.* If we follow Erasmus in suggesting that the *Regularis Informatio* is a genuine Augustinian composition and that it represents the original form of the *Rule,* prefaced by the *Obiurgatio,* why should Augustine have omitted it from the *Revisions,* in which he included a number of his letters which he considered to be treatises of general interest? Here the answer could be a desire to avoid undue publicity. The occasion of writing Letter 211 was an unhappy one—dissensions in a Catholic community at a time of Catholic rejoicing that the Roman emperor had enforced the reunion of the divided Catholic and Donatist Churches of North Africa—and nothing would be gained by advertising it. A similar consideration could have persuaded Possidius to omit it from his *Indiculum.* An argument from silence such as this cannot be pressed. There are, however, no compelling reasons why Augustine should not have made a rule, and we find the *Ordo Monasterii* and the *Praeceptum* directly attributed to him by Eugippius of Lucullanum, an admirer with a very considerable knowledge of Augustine's writings, in a document composed less than a century after Augustine's death and preserved in a manuscript of the late sixth/early seventh century (Paris, B.N. MS Lat. 12634). There is no manuscript witness for the *Regularis Informatio* earlier than the tenth century (Madrid, Escorial MS. a I 13), while the oldest complete manuscript is the Codex Turicensis of the late eleventh/early twelfth century (Zürich, MS Rheinau 89). The surviving number of early manuscripts of the *Praeceptum* renders the suggestion that it was a medieval composition untenable.[17] It also casts doubt on the possibility that the feminine form of the *Rule* antedates the masculine, though here we have to be careful, since we do not know what codices have been lost over the centuries, especially in the confusion brought about by the Vandal invasions and the subsequent persecution of the Catholic Church in North Africa. Furthermore, we cannot assume, as it was possible to do in Western Europe in recent centuries, that in the middle ages women's religious communities outnumbered those of men. Rather, they would seem to have been fewer in number,[18] which would mean that fewer copies of the *Regularis Informatio* would have been needed, and lost earlier examples therefore less readily replaced. Again, the survival of copies of the *Rule*, whether for men or for women, does not in itself prove that the owners were actually living by it—the Turicensis manuscript (Rheinau 89), for example, originally belonged to a Benedictine abbey—although they might have drawn upon it for other reasons, as did Caesarius of Arles (c.480-550) when composing his *Rule for Nuns* or Benedict of Aniane (c.750-821), the Carolingian monastic reformer, who cites the *Rule* of Augustine in his *Codex Regularum*.[19] Altogether, what is known about Augustine's *Rule* for some six centuries after his death depends on the existence of surviving codices.

So far as we can tell, it was in the late eleventh century that there occurred a sudden flowering of interest in Augustine's *Rule,* owing in large measure to the influence of the Gregorian reform movement, which sought to bring about a renewal of canonical life in the Church by the requirement of common living and a renunciation of private property on the part of canons of cathedral and collegiate churches. To that end a number of such communities, like the Canons Regular of the Lateran, whom Pope Alexander II (1061-1073) instituted in his cathedral church, adopted the *Rule* of Saint Augustine. Reforming bishops like Altmann of Passau (1065-1091), Ivo of Chartres (1090-1115) and Conrad I of Salzburg (1106-1147), founded new Augustinian houses, some of which, like the French house of Saint Ruf, near Avignon, became the mother-houses of congregations. The Premonstratensians, founded by Saint Norbert (c.1080-1134), called after their parent-monastery at Prémontré, near Laon, became a regular Augustinian order. The *Rule* of Augustine was likewise adopted, among the military orders, by the Knights of Saint John of Jerusalem and by the Teutonic Knights.

The profoundly religious society of twelfth-century Western Europe witnessed a widely-spread desire to serve God and the community in an active monastic role that was larger in scope than that of the contemplative monk or the simple parish priest. For such an aspiration the Benedictine *Rule* was unsatisfactory in that its essence was stability—a monk joined the community of a particular house and remained there, in the spirit of the Egyptian desert,[20] until death, leaving it, if at all, only in the most compelling circumstances. The way of life prescribed in the *Praeceptum,* on the other hand, while it emphasized fellowship and mutual sharing within the community and forbade any unnecessary individual absence from the monastery, was less minutely prescriptive than the Benedictine *Rule* and better adapted for a religious family wishing to pursue an active life in the service of God. In this context it may be remembered that Augustine had himself set an example by requiring that his episcopal household follow the apostolic pattern of individual poverty, thereby imposing a monastic way of life on secular priests.[21] This may help to explain how the surge of interest in community life involving active works in the eleventh and twelfth centuries led to the adoption of the Augustinian *Rule* as an alternative to the Benedictine, and to the resulting multiplication at that time of manuscript copies whose apparently unprecedented emergence later helped to persuade scholars that it was an adaptation, for practical and immediate use, of the female *Regularis Informatio* which, being attached to a recognized letter of Augustine, was deemed to be his original composition.

The impressive spread of the Augustinian *Rule* in the *Praeceptum Longius*—the *Ordo Monasterii* followed by the *Praeceptum*—in the twelfth century meant that in its practical application some modification was necessary. The problem was aired in a rather dramatic form by an appeal on the part of the Augustinian canons of Springiersbach, in the diocese of Trier, in a letter to Pope Gelasius II in 1118. The canons pointed out that they could observe neither the prescriptions of the *Ordo Monasterii* in their daily choir offices, since these had been made obsolete by liturgical development, nor its directions regarding manual labor and fasting—one meal a day, taken at three in the afternoon, was too little for German stomachs in Northern Europe. In his reply, dated 11 August 1118, the pope agreed that liturgical practice should follow established use and that manual labor and fasting should be regulated by local conditions and customs in the interest of pastoral ministry. "With regard to your offices, to manual labor, and to fasting which cannot be observed in our provinces, let suitable moderation be exercised. What must be observed, with the aid of divine grace, are the things which pertain to good morals."[22] In this context Eusebius Amort, a learned eighteenth-century Augustinian canon, suggested that, as a result of the pope's letter, the canons abandoned the use of the *Ordo Monasterii* as a whole, but placed the opening sentence—"Before all else, dearest brothers, let God be loved and then your neighbor, because these are the chief commandments which have been given us"—before the beginning of the *Praeceptum*: "You that are settled in the monastery, these are the things that we advise you to observe." However, the first appearance of this form, the *Regula recepta*, seems to have been due to Ivo of Chartres, who died in 1118, and the earliest manuscript witnesses are French or English,[23] not German, so the canons of Springiersbach cannot be regarded as having introduced it. Rather, they were apparently aware of its existence and consulted the pope on the propriety of using an abridged version of the *Rule*. Whatever the reason, the *Ordo Monasterii* appears to have been discarded fairly quickly from Augustinian use in the early twelfth century.[24]

The Ordo Monasterii

There remains, however, the question of the origin of the *Ordo Monasterii*. Eugippius of Lucullanum accepted it as a genuine compilation of Augustine and associated it with the *Praeceptum*. Pierre Mandonnet, in his famous study of

Saint Dominic, published posthumously in 1937, suggested that both the *Ordo Monasterii* and the *Praeceptum*
were the work of Augustine, the first having been composed
for his community at Thagaste and the second at Hippo
after his ordination there in 391.[25] If we accept this suggestion, it would be a plausible hypothesis that the *Regularis
Informatio* was a modification of the *Praeceptum*, made by
Augustine himself and attached to the *Obiurgatio* addressed
to the quarreling nuns about 412 as a guide to conduct,
which had worked satisfactorily at Hippo. Mandonnet's
hypothesis assumes that both the *Praeceptum* and the
Regularis Informatio are Augustinian and that the latter is a
transcription by him of the *Praeceptum*. Is this a reasonable
assumption?

So far as the *Ordo Monasterii* is concerned, it must be
recognized that it is a document of fewer than 400 words,
which are too few for any comparison with Augustine's or
any other writer's style. In any case, the *Ordo Monasterii*
differs from the *Praeceptum* not simply in style but also in
mood. It is short, being about one-fifth the length of the
Praeceptum, and is both more specific and more authoritarian in tone. It is instructive to compare and to contrast
the injunctions of the two documents on the matter of
prayer. First, the *Praeceptum* (2.1-4):

> *Persevere faithfully in prayers* (Col 4:2) at the
> appointed hours and times. In the oratory, no one
> should do anything that conflicts with its purpose,
> implied by its name.[26] Hence, if those who happen
> to be free wish to pray there outside the fixed
> hours, they should not be hindered by anyone who
> might think of doing something else there. When
> you pray to God in *psalms and hymns* (Col 3:16),

meditate in the heart on what is expressed with the voice. And sing only what is set down for you to sing. But what is not written to be sung is not to be sung.

This is something personal, addressed to the individual, not least in the warning not to sing what is not set down to be sung. We are reminded of Augustine's awareness of the temptations of what is pleasing to the ear, discussed in *Confessions* 10.33.49-50. Compare this approach with *Ordo Monasterii* 2:

> We now set down how we ought to pray and recite the psalms. At morning prayer let three psalms be said: the sixty-second, the fifth, and the eighty-ninth. At the third hour let one psalm first be said responsorially; then two antiphons;[27] a reading; and then the closing prayer. Let prayers be said in a similar fashion at the sixth and ninth hours. At lamp-lighting a responsorial psalm; four antiphons; another responsorial psalm; a reading; and then the closing prayer; and at a suitable time after lamplighting, all [the congregation] being seated, there are to be readings, and afterward the customary psalms before sleeping.

The contrast between these two passages is obvious. The first is personal and pastoral, the second formal and legislative. The *Praeceptum*, indeed, addresses itself to the individual in a manner frequently to be found in Augustine's letters and sermons; the *Ordo Monasterii* formally prescribes for the community as a whole. (It should, however, be remembered that if one is drawing up a brief list of regulations or instructions, one tends to employ a legislative form of drafting which does not reflect one's normal literary style.)

The detailed instructions for the liturgical life of the community which the *Ordo Monasterii* provides resemble those of the Benedictine *Rule* and led Dom de Bruyne to suggest in 1930 that the *Ordo* was post-Augustinian, being in fact composed by Saint Benedict for use by his first community at Subiaco.[28] This suggestion was demolished a year later by Dom Germain Morin[29] but illustrates how different an impression is made on the reader by the two compositions, the *Ordo* and the *Praeceptum*, leading to the conclusion that they can hardly be both by the same author (de Bruyne had himself provided a critical edition of the *Praeceptum* in his article of 1930).[30] Verheijen has suggested an ingenious solution to the problem. He was prepared to ascribe to Augustine the initial and final sentences of the *Ordo* but considered that the rest must have come from another hand. In view of the early association of the *Ordo* with the *Praeceptum*, he suggested that the author of the *Ordo* was probably a member of Augustine's inner circle. In this he particularly noticed Alypius, Augustine's dearest friend, who had formerly been a lawyer and had visited Jerome at Bethlehem some time before his consecration as bishop of Thagaste during the winter of 394-395. It happens that the liturgical directions in the *Ordo* strongly resemble those of the Eastern liturgies. These considerations led Verheijen to suggest that the author of the greater part of the *Ordo Monasterii* might have been Alypius.[31]

The suggestion is an attractive one, resolving, as it does, so many problems, and is mentioned as the view of some modern scholars in the article "Alypius" in the *Augustinus-Lexikon*.[32] But there are serious difficulties, the most obvious being that we have so little from the pen of Alypius that we cannot identify the style of the *Ordo Monasterii* as being possibly his. Furthermore, as George Lawless has pointed out, Augustine's education had been virtually the same as that of Alypius. As a rhetorician he would have had some knowledge of the law; he would have, on occasion, pleaded in the courts; and he would have been familiar with legal language: "There is nothing in this monastic code which would contradict Augustine's authorship."[33] It must therefore be accepted that the authorship of the *Ordo* remains a far more open, and probably insoluble, question than that of the *Praeceptum*. What is clear is that the *Ordo* appears at the very beginning of the manuscript tradition to have been associated with the name of Augustine and can therefore be reasonably regarded as part of his monastic legislation. To try to go further than this leads only to unprovable hypotheses which distort history and may easily be assumed by later generations to have been proved by continued repetition—historians, it has been fairly observed, tend to repeat one another, particularly in fields in which they have not had personal experience.

Regularis Informatio

There remains the question of the *Regularis Informatio*. On the evidence of the manuscript tradition it is difficult to regard it as the original form of the *Rule*, since its earliest codices are later in date than those of the *Praeceptum* and the stemma of its transmission is independent of the two masculine stemmata.[34] However, ever since the twelfth century there has been an opinion that the feminine form is the original, and this belief, strengthened by the endorsement of Erasmus, generally held the field until challenged by Verheijen on codicological evidence in the second half of the twentieth century.[35] Defenders of the view that the *Regularis Informatio* is the original Augustinian *Rule* have urged their case on stylistic grounds: the feminine form, they allege, reads more naturally than does the masculine, which gives the impression of having been mutilated by the excision of those passages which would not apply in a male community. Such an argument is inevitably subjective and depends, to a great degree, on personal taste and judgment and may equally well be urged against the arguments for feminine priority as for them. Thus the passage—"whether clothing or bedding, or underwear or outer garments, or a headdress—" which the *Regularis Informatio* adds to *Praeceptum* 5.2 and which Dom Lambot assumed to be integral to the passage as a whole,[36] was seen by Luc Verheijen as interrupting the thought of section 5, which is concerned with the storage of clothes in a single community wardrobe and not with their manufacture.[37] George Lawless, for his part, considered that the fourteen Latin words of the passage (*sive unde induatur sive ubi iaceat sive unde cingatur vel operiatur vel caput contegat*) introduce "a somewhat jarring note into the flow of the Latin text" and may therefore be an interpolation.[38] Such judgments are likely to be influenced by an individual's *a priori* assumptions about the document which he is criticizing. An argument which carries conviction with someone who believes in the chronological anteriority of the *Regularis Informatio* over the *Praeceptum* may seem not only unconvincing but self-refuting to another holding the opposite opinion.

If this consideration is borne in mind, many of the passages which have been seen in the past as implying a feminine community lose their force.[39] The passage in

Praeceptum 4.1—"Your clothing should not be conspicuous. You should not try to please by your clothes but by your behavior—" which has been urged as being more appropriately applied to women than to men, could equally well be accepted as a rebuke to male vanity in a society in which the quality of clothing was an indication of social status. The phrases in 8.1:—"radiating by your good life *the sweet odor of Christ*"—and in 8.2—"and so that you may be able to look at yourselves in this little book *as in a mirror*" —which are supposed to point to feminine qualities, are simply quotations from scripture (2 Cor 2:15 and Jas 1:23-26), equally applicable to both men and women. The injunction in 5.4—"Your clothes are to be washed at the discretion of the superior either by yourselves or by the fullers"— which is seen by some as being applicable only to women, assumes a male incapacity in domestic matters which need not be taken for granted in men of the fifth century who were deliberately seeking to live by their own labors after the example of Saint Paul. About the year 400 Augustine was himself to write the treatise *The Work of Monks,* in which he denounced the arguments of monks who held that prayer amounted to work and that they had, in consequence, the right to live on the offerings of others.[40] Clothes-washing, unlike needlework, does not demand any particular expertise. One can understand that nuns might be expected to make clothing for community use, but where the washing of clothes was concerned, men might do it as well as women.

Again, the *Praeceptum*'s prohibition of the secret acceptance of letters or little gifts from a woman (4.11), paralleled in the *Regularis Informatio* by "from a man," provides no indication as to which prohibition was borrowed from the other. What is curious is why this particular injunction was not dealt with in chapter 5.3, which is concerned with gifts from parents, unless it be that it was regarded as coming under the general provisions of chapter 4, regarding dealings with the opposite sex. However, the prohibition is repeated in some texts of the *Regularis Informatio* at the end of 5.3, perhaps for the sake of completeness: "If anyone conceals what is given her, let her be condemned for the theft."[41] This repetition might, of course, be due to a glossator—it does not appear in the Turicensis MS (11th 12th century), the archetype of the feminine tradition.[42]

Two other passages in the *Praeceptum* state that members of the community, if they leave the monastery on some mission, should "walk together, and when you come to your destination, stay together" (4.2) and that there should not be fewer than two or three of them, chosen by the superior and not by the person going out (5.7), in contrast to the *Regularis Informatio*, which decrees that "there should not be less than three of you." These are likewise ambiguous as regards which rule copies which. It might be argued that concern for female safety might have caused the compiler of the *Regularis Informatio* to require a party of three, while the author of the *Praeceptum* was prepared to accept a minimum of two, but equally it could be held that the compiler of the *Regularis Informatio*, faced with "two or three," preferred to play safe by opting for the larger number. In any case, the phrase "two or three" is an echo of Christ's words in the gospel, indicating his presence with his followers (Mt 18:20).

Again, the reciprocal roles assigned in chapter 7 of both the *Praeceptum* and the *Regularis Informatio* to the superior and to the presbyter-in-charge, with the presbyter-in-charge being the senior, might be interpreted as reflecting a female community which would require a male warden; but it may equally well be understood as describing the organization of Augustine's community at Hippo after Augustine himself had become bishop and could no longer exercise direct personal supervision as he had done as a presbyter. It is possible to see in the presbyter of the *Praeceptum* a member of the bishop's household charged with the general oversight of the community, as opposed to the superior's immediate responsibility, and having laison with the bishop. A similar arrangement would equally have been appropriate for a female community, and especially one where there was opposition and even downright hostility to the superior on the part of some of the members.

Finally, to see the statement of *Praeceptum* 5.2 that "all your work should be shared together" as indicating some feminine character of the community is absurd. It would be equally applicable to men as to women.

It therefore appears that the case for assuming the priority of the *Regularis Informatio* over the *Praeceptum* is not strengthened by arguments from style. If this is indeed the case, how did the *Regularis Informatio* come to be compiled?

Two facts are to be noted at the outset. First, the text of the *Regula Consensoria* is overwhelmingly in agreement with that of the *Praeceptum*, with differences only appearing when they are essential for a female congregation. Second, the *Regularis Informatio* is commonly associated in the manuscripts with the *Obiurgatio*, the rebuke for quarreling nuns, so often indeed that the two documents were generally regarded as forming a single whole, Letter 211, of which the *Obiurgatio* formed the first four sections, the *Regularis Informatio* sections 5-16. However, the earliest complete text of Letter 211 (Zürich, MS Rheinau 89) makes a break between the *Obiurgatio* and the *Regularis Informatio*—*explicit praefacio. incipit regula monialium*—which led Verheijen to suggest that an adaptation was made from the masculine rule by the monastery which had received the *Obiurgatio*:

> A copy of the *Praeceptum* could have been taken from the convent of the lay brethren [of Augustine's foundation at Hippo] to that of the nuns, transcribed by them into a feminine form with a rather passive veneration lacking creative insertions, and kept with a copy of the letter [the *Obiurgatio*] of the same author—their bishop. This nunnery (was it at Hippo? There is no certainty that it was) would then be the point of departure for the feminine tradition, the third branch of the manuscript tradition.[43]

In *La Règle de Saint Augustin*, published in 1967, Verheijen felt unable to suggest a date for the feminine transcription of the *Rule* or whether it was made before or after the writing of the *Obiurgatio*. Some years later, in the Augustine Lecture, delivered at Villanova University, Pennsylvania, in 1975 and published in 1979, he was prepared to be more definite. He had been persuaded by the suggestion of Nicolas Merlin that the *Praeceptum* might have been composed about 397, when Augustine had to abandon the monastery at Hippo for the episcopal residence. Verheijen now suggested that the transcription might have been made *before* the composition of the *Obiurgatio* on the ground that the grouping of quotations from Acts 4:32 and Ps 67:7 (68:6) which occurs in *Obiurgatio* 2 appears nowhere else in Augustine's works except in the *Praeceptum*, assumed by Verheijen to be by him. If this view is correct, it would mean that the date of the *Regularis Informatio* was before 411, the date of the Conference of Carthage with the Donatists, alluded to in

Obiurgatio 4 (*Cogitate quid mali sit ut, cum de Donatistis in unitate gaudeamus, interna schismata in monasterio lugeamus*), which would in turn push back the date of the *Praeceptum,* perhaps, as Merlin had suggested, to around 397, when Augustine, by then the sole, and very busy, bishop of Hippo, would no longer be able to concern himself with the day-to-day problems of the monastic community which he had founded and so offered his monks a general exposition of the spirituality underlying its existence, to be read to them once a week.[44]

From the manuscript evidence—and there is no other—Verheijen was persuaded, on liturgical grounds, that the feminine version of the *Ordo Monasterii* was made in Spain, before the time of Saint Isidore of Seville (c.560-636) who, he suggested, made use of it in compiling his *Rule for Nuns*.[45] Of this suggestion, no less than for Verheijen's other suggestion that the *Regularis Informatio* was made by nuns of the community to which the *Obiurgatio* was addressed, it can only be said that it cannot be more than a plausible hypothesis. The one thing which seems to be clear from the survival of manuscripts is that the *Praeceptum* antedates the *Regularis Informatio* and can reasonably, though not indisputably, be accepted as the work of Augustine himself. The Augustinian authorship of the *Ordo Monasterii* is a more questionable assumption. Mandonnet, as we have seen, considered it to be by Augustine, composed for his monastic community at Thagaste, while supposing that the *Praeceptum* was composed for the monastery of Hippo after his ordination.[46] Here again we have an attractive hypothesis which it is impossible to prove. If however the *Ordo* was composed for use at Thagaste, either by Augustine or another, this would explain the very different tone of the *Praeceptum*, had it been made, as Verheijen has suggested (see note 44), when Augustine left his garden monastery for the episcopal residence at Hippo. His brethren already had a practical schedule for their day-to-day activities. Augustine would now provide them with a more general and more spiritual guide for the monastic way of life.

Conclusions

What conclusions can be drawn from the foregoing? Let it first be once again emphasized that there is no direct information either from Augustine himself or from his biographer, Possidius of Calama, that he ever composed a rule. On the other hand, Eugippius of Lucullanum included the *Ordo Monasterii* followed by the *Praeceptum* in the rule which he composed for his own monastery, our oldest witness, preserved in Paris MS Latinus 12634, of the late-sixth to early-seventh century. Furthermore, a number of other manuscripts, of the tenth century or earlier, ascribe the *Praeceptum* to Augustine.[47] Scholarly doubts about the Augustinian authorship of the *Ordo Monasterii* would seem to be justified, but there is no compelling reason for doubting that it comes from Augustine's circle. The *Obiurgatio* would seem to be a genuine letter of Augustine and the *Regularis Informatio* could have been copied in his lifetime, though this remains only an hypothesis. However, the theology underlying the *Praeceptum*, with its emphasis on mutual sharing within the community, has a convincingly Augustinian flavor. We cannot prove the authorship of the monastic documents associated with the name of Augustine as we can prove his authorship of other works, but the evidence as a whole is decidedly in favor of regarding him as the inspirer of a way of religious life which has for centuries persuaded men and women to count themselves disciples of the bishop of Hippo.

Notes

1. It is fair to say that Verheijen initiated a new epoch in the study of the Augustinian monastic tradition.

2. See Sermons 355 (A.D. 425-426) and 356 (A.D. 426) on Augustine's idea of the episcopal household living in community. Translated by Edmund Hill, *The Works of Saint Augustine: A Translation for the 21st Century: Sermons* III,10 (New York: New City Press, 1995) 165-172, 173-183. See also Luc Verheijen, *Saint Augustine's Monasticism in the Light of Acts 4:32-35* (The Saint Augustine Lecture 1975) (Villanova University Press, 1979) 76-80.

3. *Confessions* 8.6.14-15. Translated by Maria Boulding, *The Works of Saint Augustine: A Translation for the 21st Century* I,1 (New York: New City Press, 1997) 195-196.

4. Letter 130.10.20. Translated by Roland Teske, *The Works of Saint Augustine: A Translation for the 21st Century* II, 2 (New York: New City Press, 2001).

5. Eugipii *Regula. CSEL* 87, 3-16: Maximilian Krausgruber, *Die Regel des Eugippius. Die Klosterordnung des Verfassers der Vita Sancti Severini im Lichte ihrer Quellen* (Frühes Christentum. Forschungen und Perspektiven Bd 21) (Vienna: Kultur-Verlag, 1996) 72-92.

6. See C. J. Bishko, "The Date and Nature of the Spanish 'Consensoria monachorum,'" *American Journal of Philology* 69 (1948) 377-395, who concludes: " . . . the work properly belongs to the late Visigothic period of Galician literature, between 650 and 711" (p. 395); J.C. Dickinson, *The Origins of the Austin Canons and their Introduction into England* (London: SPCK, l950), Appendix I: "The Rule of Saint Augustine: Its textual history," 254-272.

7. See George Lawless, *Augustine of Hippo and his Monastic Rule* (Oxford: Clarendon Press, 1987) 125-126, 143.

8. Verheijen, *La Règle de Saint Augustin* (Paris, 1967) I, 53 lines 1-2.

9. *Ibid.* I, 44.

10. Translated by Robert P. Russell, *The Rule of our Holy Father Saint Augustine, Bishop of Hippo* (Villanova, Penn. 1976). See Lawless, *op. Cit.*, Appendix I, 165-166.

11. Printed separately in Lawless, *op. cit.* : *Obiurgatio*, Latin and English, pp. 104-109; *Regularis Informatio* (English translation only), pp.110-118.

12. Edited by A.C. Vega, *Miscellania Giovanni Mercati* 2 (Studi e Testi l22) (Rome l946) 47-56; reprinted in *PL Supplementum* 2, 349-356.

13. Verheijen, *Règle* 1, 17; II, 180; Lawless, *op. cit.*, 65.
14. Verheijen, *Règle* II, 103-104, 187.
15. Trans. F.R. Hoare, *The Western Fathers* (London / New York : Sheed and Ward Ltd., 1954) 198.
16. Verheijen, *Saint Augustine's Monasticism,* 46.
17. For a random sample of eight manuscripts of the tenth century and earlier ascribing the *Rule* to Augustine, see Lawless, *op. cit.,* 130.
18. Thus in 1153 the Cistercian Order had 335 monasteries for men but only 20 monasteries at the most for women. See Adriaan H. Bredero, *Cluny et Cîteaux au douzième siècle. L'Histoire d'une controverse monastique* (Amsterdam and Maarssen: APA-Holland University Press, 1985) (English summary, p. 353).
19. Lawless, *Augustine of Hippo* 130, 156, 169; Benedict of Aniane in *PL* 103, 393-702.
20. Expressed in the famous saying of Antony the Great: "Just as fish die if they stay too long out of water, so the monks who loiter outside their cells or pass their time with men of the world lose the intensity of inner peace" (*The Sayings of the Desert Fathers: The Alphabetical Collection,* trans. Benedicta Ward (London and Oxford: Mowbrays, 1975), no 10, p. 2; and Abba Moses: "Go, sit in your cell, and your cell will teach you every thing," *ibid.,* no 6, p.118. See Graham Gould, *The Desert Fathers on Monastic Community* (Oxford: Clarendon Press, 1993) 139-166.
21. See *Sermon* 355,2: "I arrived at the episcopate. I saw that the bishop is under the necessity of showing hospitable kindness to all visitors and travelers; indeed, if a bishop didn't do that he would be said to be lacking in humanity. But if this custom were transferred to a monastery, it would not be fitting. And that's why I wanted to have a monastery of clergy in this bishops' residence. This then is how we live; nobody in our company is allowed to have any private property" (Hill, *Sermons* III,10, p.166); Possidius, *Life of Augustine,* 25: "The clergy and he were all fed and clothed in the same house, at the same table and from a common purse" (Hoare, *op. cit.,* 224).
22. *PL* 163, 497; Verheijen, *Règle* II,121-2; see Rudolf Arbesman, "The question of the *Regula Sancti Augustini,*" *Augustinian Studies* 1 (1970) 248-249; and Lawless, *op. cit.,* 165-166.
23. See Verheijen, *Règle* II, 117-24. Verheijen questions (p.121) Mandonnet's theory (*op. cit.* I, 149-162) that Gelasius' letter of 1118 "decapitated" the *Praeceptum Longius.*

24. See Arbesman, *art.cit. 249: "On the whole, the period during which the prescriptions of the Ordo Monasterii* were actually practiced as a norm of monastic life was rather brief."

25. Mandonnet, *Saint Dominique* (Paris 1937) II, 121-148.

26. See Benedictine *Rule*, 52.

27. It is impossible to decide how *antiphona* should be rendered, when it occurs in a document dating to the fourth or fifth century. So far as the sixth century is concerned, there is a discussion in *RB 1980: The Rule of Saint Benedict in Latin and English with Notes,* ed. Timothy Fry (Collegeville, Minn.: Liturgical Press 1981) 400-408, which brings out the difficulty of understanding the word in the light of contemporary knowledge. The word antiphon today means a short text sung before or after a psalm or canticle. In the past it could mean a psalm sung alternatively by the halves of a congregation, or by two choirs, as opposed to the responsorial style—a soloist singing a verse or half-verse of a psalm and the congregation singing the other or uttering a refrain like *Alleluia* or *Amen.* However, a suggestion has been made by Corbian Gindele (*Studia Anselmiana* 42 [1957] 171-222) that *antiphona* referred to a set of three psalms grouped together. A. de Vogüé, on the other hand, has argued that in the *Regula Magistri,* upon which the Benedictine Rule drew, *antiphona* meant *psalmus cum antiphona, t*hat is, one psalm with an antiphon. There is, however, a further consideration: that in the *Ordo Monasterii antiphona* is distinguished from *psalmus* and *psalmus responsorius*—"responsorial psalm"—or *psalmus ad respondendum*—"responsorially"—implying a kind of duet, either between two choirs or between the soloist and the congregation.

    No definite solution of the meaning of *antiphona* in the *Ordo Monasterii* is possible. It may be guessed that in the *Ordo, antiphona* means a psalm with antiphon, while *psalmus ad respondendum* is a duet; but the guess remains. See Robert Taft, *The Liturgy of the Hours in East and West. The Origins of the Divine Office and its Meaning for us Today* (Collegeville, Minn.: Liturgical Press, 2nd revised ed. 1993) 94-96 and David Hiley, *Western Plainchant: a Handbook* (Oxford: Clarendon Press, 1993) 487-494. Taft specifically discusses the *Ordo* and considers that *antiphona* means "a psalm with antiphon" (p. 95).

28. De Bruyne, "La première Règle de saint Benoît," *Revue Bénédictine* 42 (1930) 316-342.

29. Morin, "L'ordre des heures canoniales dans les monastères de Cassiodore," *RB* 43 (1931) 145-152.

30. See art. Cit., 320-326.

31. Verheijen, "Remarques sur la style de la 'Regula secunda' de Saint Augustin," *Augustinus Magister* (Paris, 1954) I, 255-263; *Règle* II,125-74.

32. By Erich Feldmann, Vol.I, Fasc. 1/2 (1986) 252.

33. Lawless, *op. cit.,* 169; Verheijen, *Règle* II, 164-9; Arbesman, *art.cit.,* 260-261.

34. Lawless, *op. cit.,* 137-139.

35. Verheijen, *Règle* II, 19 ff.; 74-80; Lawless, *op. cit.,* 145

36. Lambot, "Saint Augustin a-t-il rédigé la Règle pour moines qui porte son nom?" *Revue Bénédictine* 53 (1941) 41-58 (p. 43).

37. Verheijen, *Règle* II,74-76.

38. Lawless, *op. cit.,* 146.

39. List in Lawless, *op.cit.,* 136-137.

40. Chaucer's hunting monk in *The Canterbury Tales*, it may be recalled, took exception to Augustine's outlook—"Let Austin have his swink to him reserved"—"Let Augustine keep his labor to himself"—was his principle. For the possible identification of this sportsman with Abbot Clown of Leicester, see David Knowles, *The Religious Orders in England* Vol. II (Cambridge University Press, 1955) 185-186, 365-366.

41. And so found its way into the *Constitutiones Ordinis Fratrum S. Augustini*. See Russell, *op. cit.*, p. 3, note 9 (where for "six" in line 7 read "five").

42. See Verheijen, *Règle* I, 62, lines 165-166.

43. *Règle* II, 202.

44. Merlin, *Saint Augustin et la vie monastique* (Albi, 1933); Verheijen, *cit., Saint Augustine's Monasticism* 45-48; 70: "But now I would like to be a little more precise, and that in the light of the grouping of Acts 4:32a with Psalm 67, 7 [68, 6] in the *Obiurgatio*. I think now that the transcription may well have taken place before the sending of the *Obiurgatio*, and Saint Augustine can very well have known the presence of the feminine version of his *Rule* in the sisters' convent. This would explain perfectly why he groups in the *Obiurgatio* Acts 4: 32a with Psalm 67:7: it would be an allusion to the *Regularis Informatio* which these sisters had already made the basis of their monastic life, and in which, just as in the *Praeceptum,* Acts 4:32a and Psalm 67:7 were already grouped"; and Lawless, *op. cit.,* 145-146, 152-154.

45. *Règle* II, 209-12.

46. Mandonnet, *op.cit.* II, 104, 132-141.

47. Lawless, *op. cit.,* 130.

II

The Spirit of the Rule

In everyday language, when we speak of the spirit of an association of people or of a piece of writing, art, or music, we mean the mood and principles inspiring and conditioning the whole. In theology the word "spirituality" is often used. Since this word has a very wide range of possible meanings, it will here be defined as an orientation of the mind and will to God, expressed in an individual's life and teachings. Understood in this sense, there are a number of excellent works in English on the spirituality of the *Rule* of Saint Augustine, including Tarsicius van Bavel, *The Rule of Saint Augustine: Masculine and Feminine Versions* (1984 and 1996); Adolar Zumkeller, *Augustine's Rule. A Commentary* (1987); and Sister Agatha Mary, SPB, *The Rule of Saint Augustine. An Essay in Understanding* (1992). To these may be added Adolar Zumkeller's major study, *Augustine's Ideal of the Religious Life* (1986). The purpose of this present chapter, while not in any way seeking to ignore the enduring spirituality of the *Rule*, envisages a more directly historical approach, which will consider Augustine's monasticism as it reflects the career of the author and the conditions of his age.

Major Influences on Augustine's Monasticism

A monastic rule is, fundamentally, a set of instructions on the day-to-day life of a religious community and, as such, a prosaic document, resembling a set of school rules or barrack-room regulations. In its composition, however, the author may well reveal his personality as a Christian teacher, even if he does not—is often the case—include explicitly devotional and ascetic teaching. In the case of Augustine's monastic teaching it may be said at the outset that its spirituality is inspired by an ideal of lives offered to God in a community assembled and bound together by friendship in God, with a system of government founded on affection rather than on coercive authority. The individual who is incapable of entering into the warmth of personal relationships, with all the trials and difficulties which they can arouse, is temperamentally unsuited to an Augustinian community.

This feature is hardly surprising, given the nature of Augustine's personality and the course of his career. Whatever else he was not, he was a person who needed the support and consolation of the society of other human beings. In his youth he had been made happy by a woman's love and, however we may judge his eventual treatment of his concubine, his affection for her during most of their relationship cannot be doubted. His gratitude to his mother and his love for his son Adeodatus and pride in his achievements are plain, as is his affection for the unnamed friend whose premature death drove Augustine from Thagaste to Carthage, after his native city and family home had become a torment to him.[1] At Milan he considered, together with a circle of friends, the possibility of forming a philosophical community, pooling their financial resources.

The sincerity of our friendship would ensure that
this thing should not belong to one person and
that to another: there would be one single property
formed out of many; the whole would belong to
each of us, and all things would belong to all.[2]

This proposal anticipates, in a remarkable fashion, the
later arrangements at Thagaste and Hippo, and the fact
that the proposal foundered upon the question as to
whether wives might participate may have helped to influence the decision that these later foundations should be
monastic. The vacation spent at Cassiciacum after Augustine's conversion to Catholic Christianity in 386 marks a
further progression in his development; it included both
friends and pupils, and the only woman in the party was
Monica, "to whose merit I think I owe all that I am" (*The
Happy Life* 6).[3] In the *Soliloquies*, composed 386-388,
Augustine expresses a wish to found a religious association
which anticipates, in some degree, the community at
Thagaste, established after his return to Africa in 388,
which in turn resembles the holiday party at Cassiciacum,
now put on a permanent basis. There has been debate as to
whether Thagaste should be regarded as a monastery in the
formal sense of the word,[4] which might have been avoided if
account had been taken of the transitional and developing
condition of monasticism in the West in the late fourth
century. Augustine's writings give no evidence of any
formal organization at Thagaste, such as became the norm
in later monasticism, in East and West alike, though this
does not prove that none existed, and he certainly considered himself a *servus Dei*—a slave of God—at this time.[5]
However, the impression of informality, of the coming
together of like minds, remains. From what Augustine

himself says, it would appear that he was contemplating establishing the community of Thagaste on a more formal footing when he visited Hippo in 391, with wholly unforeseen consequences.[6] Forced by his ordination to give up the immediate day-to-day oversight of the monastery, and then required by his succession to Valerius as bishop of Hippo in or around 395 to move out of it and to reside in the bishop's house, Augustine turned his episcopal household into a monastery (the first monastic chapter in history?) and required each cleric to donate his possessions to the common purse. At the end of his life he made no will, since he did not regard himself as owning any property; what he possessed belonged to the church of Hippo.[7]

Behind this enthusiasm for the monastic life lies the inspiration provided by the description of the monks of Egypt that Ponticianus gave the morning of the day of Augustine's conversion. According to Augustine's own account, he had, up to that time, been entirely ignorant of monasticism, of Saint Antony, the first monk, and of the monastery outside Milan, patronized by Saint Ambrose.[8] He was, he says, morally in a state of indecision, which he likens to that of a sleeper, unable to rouse himself from a state of somnolence.[9] Ponticianus followed his account of the monks of the Egyptian desert with a story of himself and three of his colleagues on duty at Trier, one of whom came on a hermitage and there discovered a copy of *The Life of Antony,* which led him, on the spot, to abandon the imperial service and to become a hermit—a decision in which he persuaded his colleagues to join.[10] This account of an immediate conversion initiated the crisis which caused Augustine, the same day, to make the decision, in the garden at Milan, to follow the way of continence to the greater glory of God.

There are, then, two major influences determining
Augustine's monasticism: a lifelong need for human
companionship; and enthusiasm for the monastic way of
life, inspired by Ponticianus' narration on the day of his
conversion. In order, however, to appreciate how these are
expressed in his monastic legislation, we have to examine
the documents principally involved, in order to consider
how they may be regarded as expressing Augustine's spirituality.

The Praeceptum *(Rule for Men)*

First, the *Rule for Men*, called the *Praeceptum* by Luc
Verheijen which, following his researches, is here accepted
as the work of Augustine himself. It is impossible to date
this document from external evidence, since Augustine
does not mention it in the *Revisions* nor in any other of his
writings. However, a reference to the *praepositus* (superior)
of the monastery and to the *presbyter* (priest), who are
responsible for the well-being of the community (7.1*),
suggests that it was compiled when Augustine was bishop of
Hippo, perhaps about the time when Bishop Valerius had
died and Augustine was compelled to move into the
bishop's house, as a guide for the community, now that he
was not immediately on hand to guide it. Hence, perhaps,
the requirement that it should be read to the community
once a week (8.2). This document is the major source for
understanding Augustine's monasticism.

The *Rule for Women,* called by Verheijen the *Regularis
Informatio,* is a feminized version of the *Rule for Men,* with
certain additions applicable to a women's community. A

---

* All references are to the *Rule* (*Praeceptum*) unless otherwise noted.

succession of scholars has seen the *Rule for Women* as the original version of the Augustinian *Rule* and regarded the masculine form as being an adaptation from it. Whether this theory is correct or not—and the assumption of this essay is that it is not—is, however, irrelevant to discussion of the spirituality of the *Rule,* since the feminine version differs from the masculine only in gender and a few short additions, which do not affect the theme.

Augustine's *Letter of Rebuke* for quarreling nuns, called by Verheijen the *Obiurgatio,* composed after 411,[11] has in earlier printings preceded and been joined to the *Rule for Women* and been numbered Letter 211. It is addressed to a community of women over whom Augustine's sister, now dead, had previously presided, where there was opposition to her successor. The discontent was related in some way to the priest of Augustine's household who was the bishop's liaison officer with the community. It has been suggested that, when Augustine wrote his letter reprimanding the malcontents, he may have added a feminized version of the *Rule for Men* to provide a pattern of living which would help to ensure future harmony. Verheijen did not find this suggestion convincing, but in any case the *Rebuke*, not being in itself a rule, can only serve to indicate the spirit of Augustine's monastic legislation, with its emphasis on mutual love and respect for the superior. The preceding letter, Letter 210, is relevant here, if not directly connected with the incident.[12]

Regulations for a Monastery, called *Ordo Monasterii* by Verheijen, is the shortest, and also the most puzzling, of our four documents. Although many scholars question or deny its Augustinian authorship, it is found preceding the *Rule for Men* in the earliest known manuscript (Paris, B.N. MS Latinus 12634 of the sixth-seventh century). It was associ-

ated and apparently used with the *Rule for Men* down to the
twelfth century, when its use was abandoned as being
incompatible with liturgical changes in the Western
Church and the physical demands of life in Northern
Europe, in contrast to those of the Mediterranean region.
Nevertheless, it contrived to have its first sentence—
"Before all else, dear brothers, let God be loved, and then
the commandments which have been given us"—transferred as a preface to the *Rule for Men,* where it remains as
part of the official version used by Augustinians.[13] Therefore, whether composed by Augustine or by some unknown
author, it can be fairly regarded as coming from the Augustinian milieu.

Regulations for a Monastery is a much shorter document
than the *Rule for Men* (less than 400 words) and differs in
tone, being more prescriptive and less hortatory. This has
led to doubts about its Augustinian authorship. Verheijen
suggested as the author Augustine's friend Alypius, who
remained at Thagaste after Augustine's forced ordination
at Hippo in 391. Shortly before Augustine's consecration as
bishop of Thagaste in the winter of 394-395, Alypius
visited Jerome at Bethlehem and could there have become
acquainted with Greek monastic offices, thereby providing
the pattern for the horarium of *Ordo* 2. However, the fact
that Augustine's community at Hippo had already been
established for three years before Alypius' visit to the East
suggests that his gift would have been a somewhat belated
one. How had Augustine's monastery managed during the
previous three years?

The fact is that all explanations can only be conjectural.
It is, however, to be noted that there is no contradiction
between the *Ordo* and the *Rule for Men,* and that the former
could have provided a formal pattern of life for Augustine's

monks[14] while the latter could represent Augustine's reflections on its implications, when he finally moved out of the
monastery for the bishop's house. One point is worth
remarking. *Ordo* 6 says of the brethren: "Let them obey
faithfully. Let them honor their father next to God and
submit to their superior (*praepositus*) as becomes saints."
The *Rule for Men* 7.1 declares: "You should obey your superior as you would a father with respect to his office, lest you
offend God who is in him." The situation envisaged in the
Rule for Men seem to pertain to the time after Augustine had
become bishop of Hippo: the community is now led by the
superior and Augustine's place taken by a presbyter, who
represents the non-resident bishop. But who is the "father"
of the *Ordo*? Is he Augustine himself, the spiritual father of
the community? A clue may be provided by Augustine's
anti-Manichean work, *The Catholic Way of Life and the Mani-
chean Way of Life*, written in 388. It was begun at Rome,
where Augustine passed the time between his mother's
death and his eventual return to Africa. In the first book of
the work, Augustine spoke with enthusiasm of the monastic
life with a knowledge perhaps gained from Jerome's letter to
the Roman virgin Eustochium (Letter 22), or from circles at
Rome acquainted with Jerome, or from both. In this letter
Jerome describes a monastic organization of the Pachomian
pattern, with the monks divided into groups of ten, each
headed by a dean (*decanus*), with the deans responsible to a
father (*pater*).[15] In *The Catholic Way of Life* 1.31.67 Augustine describes a similar arrangement:

> These deans, administering everything with great
> care, and promptly performing whatever that life
> demands on account of the weakness of the body
> [like food, drink, or clothing], themselves however

have rendered account to one whom they call
father (*pater*). These fathers are not only most holy
by their morals but are of the highest doctrinal
excellence and of highest competence in all matters. They take counsel with those whom they call
their sons without any pride, thanks to their great
authority in giving commands and the great desire
of their sons to obey.[16]

One might guess that at Hippo in 391 Augustine was
regarded as the spiritual father of the community, but since
he was, as a presbyter, at the service of the bishop, a
praepositus would be required for the day-to-day administra-
tion of the community. Whether there had been a superior
at Thagaste we cannot know; but at the time of his fateful
visit to Hippo in 391 Augustine apparently had plans to
establish a monastery in that neighborhood, presumably on
more formal lines than those observed at Thagaste.[17] His
unexpected and undesired ordination to the presbyterate
meant that, although permitted to live with his fellow
monks, he was at Bishop Valerius' disposal and could only
give a limited amount of time to his foundation. This would
have rendered the institution of a permanent superior
necessary, with Augustine at hand to advise him on difficult
matters.

If this chain of hypotheses is acceptable—and we are
working in a realm of hypotheses—then the *Ordo* might
have been composed, by Augustine or another, at the beginning of his time as presbyter of Hippo, to provide a general
outline of the régime of the monastery. When however he
was constrained to leave the monastery for the episcopal
residence and would thereafter deal with the community
largely through one of his priests, he could well have been

moved to compose the *Rule for Men* for his monks, not as a rule in itself but as a set of reflections inspired by the *Ordo*, with certain practical injunctions, like custody of the eyes, added in the hope of encouraging that progress to salvation spoken of in *Ordo* 11. The *Rule* would be, in some sense, a commentary on the *Ordo*, and thus the two would have been associated, to be published together by Eugippius of Lucullanum in the late fifth or early sixth century.

With these considerations in mind, it seems reasonable to regard the *Ordo* as a significant witness to Augustine's monastic spirituality as expounded in the *Rule for Men*. Both documents are in substantial agreement. There is, however, one item in the *Ordo* which may seem to be at variance with the spirit of the *Rule*, which needs to be considered at this point: the provision for corporal punishment for the disobedient in *Ordo* 10:

> If anyone does not strive to carry out these things with all his strength, aided by the Lord's mercy, but stubbornly refuses to accept them and after being warned once and again does not amend his ways, let him know himself to be subject to the monastic discipline as may be fitting. If however his age shall be such [as to make it appropriate], he may even be whipped.

We have only one example of such punishment being inflicted, recorded in one of Augustine's letters, probably written in 422,[18] when a young monk, a former secretary (*notarius*) of Augustine, was found by the superior of the monastery chatting with some nuns at an inappropriate time and was beaten (*plagis coercitur*), a punishment which caused him to abandon the monastery.[19] It is difficult to draw any particular conclusions from this incident. If there were children in the monastery, as the words "If however his age shall be such, he may even be whipped" seem to imply, this would simply have been in accordance with the accepted methods of centuries of classical education. Horace, in the first century B.C., remembered his flagellating schoolmaster, Orbilius (*Orbilius plagosus*). Four centuries later the Burgundian professor, Decimus Magnus Ausonius, in a poem addressed to his grandson about to start school, speaks of classroom beatings as a matter of course, with the rather dispiriting consolation: "Your parents went through this and they survived."[20] Augustine himself had painful memories of his own school days and of the way in which his father and mother were amused by his whippings,[21] yet in *The City of God* he takes corporal punishment as a necessary part of education:

> What is the purpose of the pedagogue, the schoolmaster, the stick, the strap, the birch, and all the means of discipline? By such means, as holy scripture teaches, the flanks of a beloved child must be beaten, for fear that he may grow up untamed and become so hardened that he is almost, or even completely, beyond discipline,

and he speaks of "the punishments of childhood, without which the young cannot learn the lessons their elders wish them to be taught."[22] Such assumptions find little favor with educationalists in the twenty-first century; but for many generations they were taken for granted—Saint Benedict recommended that choir boys who made mistakes in reciting the psalter should be whipped, whereas older offenders were only required to make satisfaction by an act of public penitence.[23] This is the outlook of the *Ordo*.

Accordingly, we can regard the teachings of the *Regulations for a Monastery,* however limited its scope may be, as being complementary to the *Rule for Men* and informed by the same underlying spirituality. The *Rule* opens with the declaration that the community should live in *unity of spirit* (Ps 68:6) and have *one soul and one heart* (Acts 4:32) centered on God (1.2). For this reason, "no one should call *anything* his own, but you should have *everything in common*" (Acts 4: 32; 35) (1.3-4; see *Ordo* 4). The common property of the monastery should be distributed by the superior not equally but according to the individual need (1.3; see *Ordo* 4). Every new entrant to the community is required to give his possessions to the common fund, so as to ensure fraternal equality (1.4). Former positions in society must be forgotten; thus poor recruits should not glory in their association with people who, in the world, would have been their social superiors (1.6) nor, if their living conditions in the monastery are better than those outside, should they take them for granted (1.5). On the other hand, monks who come to religion from the upper classes, having made a generous contribution to the community's economic resources from their riches, are not to patronize those of their brethren who are of humble origins and brought in little or nothing (1.7).

All this may seem obvious enough; but it is essential to remember the stratification of Roman society: class distinction was marked in a way that has sharply decreased in post-industrial society.[24] There was, of course, social mobility in the Roman world; but the gulf between the aristocrat and the citizen, and still more that between the free man and the slave, who could on occasion be treated with great cruelty by the owner,[25] was very marked. Augustine's *Rule* seeks to end all such distinction in a community of religious; but it nevertheless assumes that persons who come to the monastery from the lower ranks of society will be physically able to live more austerely than rich recruits (3.3-4).

This assumption is well illustrated by a story in the *Sayings of the Desert Fathers* about an aristocratic monk, probably Arsenius, a former courtier at Rome, who came to the wilderness of Scete at the end of the fourth century, bringing with him a slave to minister to him and furnishing his cell a good deal more comfortably than was usual in the desert. An Egyptian peasant turned monk, who visited him, was inwardly scandalized by the old man's apparent self-indulgence. The former courtier, however, argued that his way of life, comfortable as it might seem to a former herdsman, represented a much greater degree of self-sacrifice than anything that his critic had experienced in coming to Scete as a monk. This argument convinced the Egyptian, who exclaimed: "Woe is me! For after so much hardship in the world I have found ease, and what I did not have before, that I now possess, while after so great ease you have come to humility and poverty."[26] Whether Augustine had heard this story of Arsenius we do not know—he certainly knew of the Egyptian hermit, John of Lycopolis, and his promise of victory to the Emperor Theodosius I[27]— but it provides an admirable illustration of his attitude: the poor are better able to bear hardship than the rich. Nevertheless, in the case of illness, those who have come from conditions of extreme poverty are to have the same consideration as those who were formerly rich, even though it is assumed that they will, when recovered, revert to their more strenuous way of life (3.5).

Augustine's notion of fraternity, then, does not necessarily involve equality of treatment at all times. He takes seriously the text of Acts 4:35: *Distribution was made to each as any had need.*[28] Needs differ, and some individuals do not require as much as others. Underlying and informing this principle, however, is Augustine's concern for the spiritual well-being of his monks. Those who were formerly poor were not to give way to vanity because they now lived on equal terms with their former superiors (1.6) but, on the other hand, those former social superiors had to forget the riches which they gave up when they entered the monastery (1.7). In both cases there lurks the danger of pride, for Augustine the supreme sin. "Every other vice prompts people to do evil deeds; but pride lies in ambush even for good deeds in order to destroy them" (1.7). It is this consideration which governs the *Rule's* provisions for the care of the sick. Every patient should be given the best treatment suitable for him, but those formerly poor "when they have recovered their strength . . . should resume their own more fortunate way of life, since the less God's servants need, the more fitting it is. . . . It is better to need less than to have more" (3.5).

Augustine sums up his teaching about life in community in section 1.8: "Therefore you should all live *united in mind and heart* (Acts 4:32) and should in one another honor God (Rom 15:6), whose temples you have become (2 Cor 6:16)." It is the friendship among individuals, sanctified by their association in the monastic community, which enables them to have *one soul and one heart* (Acts 4:32) centered on God (1.2); and it is this unity which enables them to honor God in one another (1.8). Clearly, this process is—or should be—a progress, and a continuing one. The monk does not become perfect by entering a community and Augustine has to provide for possible quarreling (6.1) and to require apologies for actions which give pain to others (6.2); but if the will to continue in the common service of God persists, then the hope of growth in holiness remains. This is the principle underlying the opening of *Regulations for a Monastery,* now prefaced to the *Rule for Men* in the official version of the *Rule:* "Before all else, dearest brothers, let God be loved and then your neighbor, because these are the chief commandments which have been given us" (*Ordo* 1).

Augustine's frequent citation of Acts 4:32 as the basis for his monastic theology has been the subject of a detailed discussion by Luc Verheijen, who thinks that Augustine understands the phrase, "the multitude of believers had but *one soul and one heart* centered on God," as signifying "above all a movement tending toward God, a movement *in Deum.*"[29] Augustine was not, of course, the first monastic theologian to appeal to the text—it is, indeed, rather an obvious one;[30] but he understood it in a particular way: as emphasizing the importance of the communal character of the monastery, not simply as an association of monks living under a common rule but as a band of brothers held together by love of God and love of each other. To grasp the nature of Augustine's thinking, we may contrast it with another rule, *The Rule of the Master,* drawn up in Italy in a region near Rome in the first quarter of the sixth century, rather more than a hundred years after Augustine's *Rule for Men. The Rule of the Master* is famous as a major source of the Benedictine Rule and the attitude of its compiler is therefore of the greatest interest, especially when compared with Augustine's. Of the Master's attitude to cenobitism a leading authority, Dom Adalbert de Vogüé, has noted two characteristics:

> First, our author shows almost no interest in the relationships of the brothers among themselves.

The only important thing in his eyes is the "vertical" relation uniting the brothers to their superiors, the deans and, above all, the abbot. This is the sense in which the monastery was for him a school, a place where disciples received the instruction of qualified masters. "Horizontal" relationships, binding the disciples to one another, are scarcely discernible. Apparently such relationships were accorded no appreciable role in the formation of souls.

A second characteristic, related to the first, is the Master's lack of interest in the community as such. Seldom do we come across a remark about the communitarian aspect of the renunciation of property or of prayer. . . . The monastery was seldom viewed as a society of charity in the sharing of goods and the union of hearts on the model of the primitive church and in the image of the Trinity. First and foremost the monastery was a school, an institution where individuals were assembled for a time for educational purposes . . . without any provision or even possibility for deepening relations very much.[31]

The contrast depicted here between the Master's monasticism and Augustine's could hardly be greater. The Master stood in a tradition which found inspiration in the "master and disciple" relationship of the Egyptian desert,[32] in which the disciple put himself under an experienced monk and was expected to obey him without question, however extravagant his commands might be. Augustine, in contrast, starts from the bond of friendship among Christian souls, united by love of God and of one's neighbor. As a result the Augustinian *Rule* is not, and cannot be, authoritarian in the way that *The Rule of the Master* and the Benedictine *Rule* are authoritarian. The Augustinian superior is not styled—perhaps deliberately not styled—an abbot. The monks are exhorted to honor and to obey him (7, 1; *Ordo* 6), but he is more commonly seen as one ministering to the needs of his fellows: "If anything is needed, their superior should take care of it" (1.3, 5.3, 5.4; *Ordo* 7;). He has authority (4.9, 5.5, 7.1-2) and should exercise it in such a way that it is not weakened by excessive humility on his part (6.3). However, he should not take pleasure in having authority but rather be glad to be able to care for his brethren, seeking their love rather than their fear, always remembering that he will have to render an account of his stewardship to God (7.3). Reciprocally, the members of the community should obey the superior as they would a father, with respect for his office (7.1),[33] and by their obedience show their concern for him, since the higher the position held, the greater the responsibility of the one holding it (7.4).

Nothing is said in either *Regulations for a Monastery* or the *Rule for Men* about how the superior comes to hold his position or how a successor is to be appointed. These omissions suggest that both documents were intended for the use of an existing community and do not offer general directions for others. The superior is already in office, whether appointed by Augustine or elected by the community, and no provision is made for a change in this situation. The same applies to *Obiurgatio* 4: the superior, formerly serving under Augustine's sister, the previous superior, has now succeeded her in office; but how she was appointed we are not told.

Following the declaration of the reason for the monastery's existence comes a discussion of prayer, which is a primary, though not the only, duty of the community. *"Persevere faithfully in prayer* (Col 4:2) at the appointed hours and times" (2.1). *Regulations for a Monastery* 2 gives directions for the Daily Office.[34] The *Rule* does not do so, presumably seeing no need to repeat what has already been set down. Augustine, however, insists that the oratory of the house should be what its name implies: a house of prayer, so that anyone who wishes to pray when not otherwise occupied should be able to do so without disturbance. What form such private prayer should take is not discussed. In his *Soliloquies*, composed in 387 soon after his conversion, Augustine opens his attempt to know God and himself through reasoning by a very lengthy prayer, in a style not unlike that of the opening of the *Confessions,* full of invocations, which give it something of the tone of a litany.[35] A quarter of a century later, in his letter to the widow Proba, Augustine is concerned to understand prayer as a continual desire for God, an orientation of the will, even when we are engaged in activities which do not permit us to use words.[36] We use the spoken words of the offices at certain intervals, but that unceasing prayer, commanded by the apostle: *Pray without ceasing* (1 Thes 5:17), is a constant desire for God. In his *Homily on the First Letter of John* 4.6, Augustine declares that the whole life of the good Christian is a holy desire, but this does not demand loquacity on the part of the suppliant, and Augustine refers to the short ejaculatory prayers of the Egyptian desert, which permit the monk to remain alert and not be weighed down with superfluous locution:

Much talking in prayer is to burden the necessary
petition with superfluous words; but much praying is to press him to whom we pray with a continual and devout stirring of the heart. For often the
matter is effected more by groans than by words.
For God places *our tears in his sight, and our groaning
is not hid from* him who created all things by his
Word and has no need of human words.[37]

Like other patristic and later writers, Augustine regards
the Lord's Prayer as the model of our praying and sees its
clauses as a test for the lawfulness of our petitions.[38] He
takes it for granted that we will pray for others, our friends,
our enemies, and the departed.[39] It has been suggested that
his injunction that the oratory is to be used for no other
purpose than as a house of prayer may have reflected the
limited accommodation at his original monastery at
Thagaste;[40] but it may equally stem from a simple desire
that there should be somewhere in the monastery where the
individual could pray without disturbance, when free to do
so. Opinion has always varied as to whether churches
should be kept for worship alone or whether they may, and
indeed should, be available for other activities; but there is
no question that many people derive comfort from having
available a place entirely set apart for prayer and medita-
tion, without any danger of disturbance.

The *Regulations* provide a pattern for the daily worship of
the community as a whole, which is not repeated in the
Rule. Augustine does, however, give brief directions about
the minds of the worshipers: reflective attention to what is
being sung (2.3), and the need to confine singing to what is
actually prescribed to be sung (2.4). The first injunction
may seem to be obvious, in view of the tendency, common

down the ages, to allow music to enjoy an ever-increasing role in worship, so that it begins to usurp the precedence of the words said, thereby transforming public worship from being an affair involving every individual worshiper into an operatic performance in which only a few participate. It may be that it was with this possibility in mind that Augustine decreed a limit to musical performance. African Christians, Catholic and Donatist alike, seem to have had a liking for singing,[41] and Augustine wanted to set bounds to this tendency; but there may also have been an element of personal concern. He has recorded in the *Confessions* the wonderful effect on him of the singing in Ambrose's cathedral at Milan in the days which followed his baptism.[42] But he also recognized, from the perspective of a decade, when he actually wrote the *Confessions*, that he had been too much influenced by the music, a bondage from which God had set him free.

> At times it seems to me that I am paying [these melodies] more honor than is their due, because I am aware that our minds are more deeply moved to devotion by those holy words that are sung, and more ardently inflamed to piety, than would be the case without singing. I realize that all the varied emotions of the human spirit respond in ways proper to themselves to a singing voice and a song, which arouse them by appealing to some secret affinity. Yet sensuous gratification, to which I must not yield my mind for fear it grow languid, often deceives me; not content to follow meekly in the wake of reason, in whose company it has gained entrance, sensuous enjoyment often essays to run ahead and to take the lead. And so in this

respect I sin inadvertently, and only realize it
later.[43]

These words help to explain Augustine's exhortations in
the *Rule*. He is constantly concerned that beautiful created
things should not turn us from the pursuit of the true
Beauty, which is God, so that we *enjoy* what we only ought
to *use*. Augustine is very far from being an extreme ascetic,[44]
but there is in his thought an underlying asceticism, based
upon his essentially eschatological outlook: we are jour-
neying to God, and everything which distracts us from that
journey is to be dispensed with.[45] This view would, of
course, be endorsed by most Christian teachers; but not all
would understand it as uncompromisingly as does Augustine.[46]

One further detail about the prayer life of Augustine's
community, at once obvious and at the same time easily
overlooked, is to be noticed. In the *Rule for Men* he says:
"Therefore when you are in company together, in church or
elsewhere where women are also present, you should protect one another's modesty" (4. 6).

The point here is that while the monastery has an oratory
for the daily office and for private prayer, the monks will
attend the public worship of the cathedral of Hippo—they
form part of the whole diocesan family. Despite the presence of Augustine as a presbyter, or of his presbyter after he
had become bishop, the monks are to come to communion
on Sunday like everybody else. Monasteries are, and will
remain, associations of laymen among whom the presence
of an ordained minister is the exception and not the rule.
The monk is a lay Christian—a dedicated and devout Christian, it is true, but not separated by holy orders from the
majority of his fellow Christians.

To the duty of prayer in the monastery, Augustine adds study. *Regulations for a Monastery 3* lays it down that three hours a day are to be devoted to reading. The *Rule* adds a practical detail: library hours are to be observed and books—unlike clothes and footware (5.11)—are not to be issued outside those hours (5.10). These regulations presuppose a literate community and no provision is made for instructing an illiterate recruit. We can only assume that such persons were given the necessary instruction. Since individual recruits would contribute their own books to the monastic library, which Augustine would no doubt have steadily augmented by his own writings, we can assume that the collection as a whole would have been a relatively large one.[47]

Food

The third section of the *Rule* is concerned with the diet of the monastery, but only as it were in passing. The brethren seem to have eaten twice a day: a light meal at noon, the main meal at about 3 p.m. On fast days, those in good health ate only in the evening. Unlike *The Rule of the Master,* Augustine gives no material details about the character of the food or the way in which it was prepared—did the brethren take turns in serving in the kitchen, or was there a full-time cook? We know that Augustine , as a bishop, was a vegetarian, although meat was available for guests and inva-lids, and that he always had wine on his table.[48] *Regulations for a Monastery 7*, however, lays down that wine may be served on Saturdays and Sundays to those who want it, which implies that only water was available on weekdays. Augustine introduces his remarks on food and drink by urging his readers to discipline themselves by fasting, and forbidding any food to be taken before the midday meal, except in the case of illness (3.1). He enjoins reading during meals (3.2; *Ordo* 7) and does not appear to provide any opportunity for conversation, though as a bishop the rules of hospitality constrained him to allow it, while forbidding any malicious gossip.[49] The rather jejeune treatment of diet in the *Rule* (3.1-2) leads to a long passage (3.3-5) warning against any resentment being shown to those whose former manner of life may mean that they need a special diet, not required by those who in the past had lived more roughly. If Augustine here seems to make rather heavy weather of what might seem a reasonable injunction against envy, it is necessary to remind ourselves afresh of the rigid boundaries of class distinction in late Roman society and the psychological effect upon those who, being born in a lower order, found themselves members of a community in which everyone was theoretically equal but where some appeared to be more equal than others because of their social origins. Conceivably, Augustine's concern might reflect the actual circumstances of the monastery of Hippo. The community at Thagaste was presumably composed of people from Augustine's own circle—intellectual, educated, and drawn from the upper middle classes. If there had been an enlargement in the community at Hippo, with an influx of lower-class members,[50] tension might have arisen between them and their former social superiors.

However, the essential element in Augustine's words is his reiteration of what he had already said about possessions (1.4-7): everyone who enters the monastery must place himself on an equal footing with everybody else. Certainly, account is to be taken of individual needs: some people are weaker than others and need special consideration. Augustine considered that such special consideration would generally be needed by recruits from the higher orders of society: the poor will be stronger from their previous way of life and, if taken ill, will recuperate faster; during convalescence, however, they must be given the best possible food, because

> recent illness has made necessary for them what a former way of life has made necessary for the rich. But when they have recovered their strength they should resume their own more fortunate way of life, since the less God's servants need, the more fitting it is. (3. 5)

Augustine's sympathies appear to be with the rich, who have made a greater sacrifice than the poor, in material terms, by entering the monastery (3. 4); but his desire is to encourage all his monks to greater asceticism: "It is better to need less than to have more" (3. 5). Augustine never recommended the extreme asceticism, for instance, of the Syrian monks exemplified by Symeon Stylites; but equally, he did not want the monastic life to be a comfortable one.

Clothing

This consideration perhaps inspires his next, brief, injunction: "Your clothing should not be conspicuous. You should not try to please by your clothes but by your behavior" (4.1). This may seem obvious to later readers, but the situation was otherwise in the first monastic centuries where the word "monk" embraced a wide range of meaning—Pelagius, for example, was called a monk by his contemporaries, though he does not appear to have had any connection with a monastery. The classic garb of the desert monk was the sheepskin (*melotes*) which, if not beautiful, was certainly conspicuous. As a monastic bishop, Augustine would have worn a long linen tunic and over that a *birrus,* a kind of cloak, and he was embarrassed if an admirer tried to present him with an expensive one. Instead, he asked for the sort of garment which he could give to a brother.[51] This could suggest, but no more than suggest, that his monks were dressed rather like their bishop. When Augustine comes to discuss the storage arrangements for the community's clothes he gives no indication of their color or cut, but only encourages the sharing, and

> if . . . someone complains that he has received something that is not as good as what he had before, and considers that it is beneath his dignity to wear what another brother has worn, this shows how far you are lacking in holiness in the holy interior clothing of your heart, since your dispute is about the clothing of the body (5.1).

This indifference to detail contrasts with the long chapter in *The Rule of the Master* 81 which describes the clothing and shoes to be worn by the monks in both summer and winter. For Augustine, a willingness to share clothing is a measure of a monk's humility, although we hope that, like Saint Benedict at a later date, he took care that the garments issued fitted the wearer.[52] Yet, the indiscriminate issue of clothing does not, in itself, preclude vanity on the part of the recipient of a garment which, in his opinion, suits him, and *The Rule of the Master* forcefully provides for this:

. . . if it is seen that any brother is dressing up and taking too much pleasure in his appearance, let what he has be immediately taken from him by his deans and given to another, and that of the other to him.[53]

We may then interpret Augustine's advice that "your clothing should not be conspicuous" as forbidding excess in the direction either of elegance or of indifference to appearance. He would have agreed with Saint Jerome's advice: "Avoid somber garments as much as bright ones. Showiness and slovenliness are alike to be shunned; the one savors of vanity, the other of boastfulness."[54]

Leaving the Monastery

The next section of the *Rule* (4.2-4.11) is concerned with a monk's behavior if he has to leave the monastery for any reason. In the first place, Augustine insists that monks should not go out singly:

When you go out, walk together; and when you get to your destination, stay together. In walking, in standing and in all your movements, nothing should be done that might cause offense to anyone who sees you; everything should be in keeping with your holy state. (4.2-3)

This parallels *Ordo* 8, which decrees that no one is to eat and drink outside the monastery without permission, "for such behavior does not accord with monastic discipline." Monks are to keep a distance from the world without making an exhibition of themselves.

This provision applies particularly to dealings with women. In discussing Augustine's injunctions it is important to bear in mind the perspective of his age regarding relations between the sexes. There is undoubtedly a strain of exaggerated asceticism in early Christianity which is disconcerting to most contemporary Christians. Furthermore—and this may seem even more distasteful today— there is Augustine's requirement that unseemly behavior in a brother, such as making eyes at a woman, should, if it is not amended, be reported to the superior. This seems like encouraging tattling, a particularly unpleasant activity, out of keeping with honorable behavior and a dedicated Christian life. However, careful examination of what Augustine lays down suggests that his rules are more reasonable than might appear at first glance.

At the outset, it must be borne in mind that Augustine's monks are spiritual brothers who, by reason of their profession, are required to have a common love and concern for one another.

> If your brother had a wound in his body, which he wished to keep secret for fear of medical treatment, would it not be cruel to keep silent and compassionate to make it known? How much more, then, ought you to report him so that he should not suffer from a more terrible festering, that of the heart. (4.8)

Monks are expected to watch over one another, morally as well as physically (4.6), and once the *Rule* had been completed, every individual should have heard the warning read out weekly (8.2), while before then we can be sure that it would have been frequently repeated by Augustine in conferences with the brethren.

Even if your gaze chances to fall on a woman you should not stare at her. There is no rule forbidding you to see women when you go out, but to attract or encourage their attention is wrong. Nor is it only by touch and strong feelings that desire (*concupiscentia*) for women is aroused but also by the way of looking. You cannot claim to have pure minds if you have impure eyes, for an impure eye is the messenger of an impure heart. (4.4)

There can be no doubt about the text underlying this passage. It is Matthew 5:28: " *I say to you that everyone who looks at a woman lustfully* (ad concupiscendam eam*) has already committed adultery with her in his heart.*" Making eyes at a girl may seem a venial sin, but Augustine's authority was the words of Christ himself, and the offenders were monks, dedicated to chastity, and not young men looking for wives. Furthermore, there was always the possibility that what began as a mild flirtation might develop into a serious attachment.

The procedure for dealing with a brother behaving improperly is once again dictated by scripture (Dt 19:15; Mt 18:16; 2 Cor 13, 1; 1 Tm 5:19).

> *If your brother sins against you, go and tell him his fault, between him and you alone. If he listens to you, you have gained your brother. But if he does not listen, take one or two others along with you, that every word may be confirmed by the evidence of two or three witnesses. If he refuses to listen to them, tell it to the church, and if he refuses to listen even to the church, let him be to you as a Gentile and a tax collector.* (Mt 18:15-17)

These dominical injunctions determine the form of Augustine's legislation. An offender, when detected, is to be rebuked privately and, if he reforms, the matter is ended. If, however, he continues to offend, then the superior should be informed (4.9), so that he may use his authority to reprimand the sinner. If, however, he denies the charge, then other monks, the *two or three witnesses*, should be asked to watch him, so that in a final confrontation there will be evidence available to refute his denials in the presence of the superior or the priest, who constitute a court—the "church" of Matthew 18:17.

Accordingly, Augustine's directions regarding the behavior of his monks toward women are biblically inspired and more reasonable than might appear on first reading. His general principle is that "nothing should be done which might cause offense to anyone who sees you; everything should be in keeping with your holy state" (4.3). Christian opinion required a high degree of deportment in religious persons, especially in their dealings with the opposite sex, and Augustine's approach was a reasonable one: "There is no rule forbidding you to see women when you go out, but to attract or encourage their attention is wrong" (4. 4). This attitude is in marked contrast to the misogyny so often found in the Egyptian desert, where many monks would shrink from or even avert their gaze from a woman. In one instance, a monk met some nuns and turned aside from the road. Their abbess—admirable soul!—said to him: "If you had been a perfect monk you would not have looked so closely as to see that we were women."[55] Augustine took a more reasonable view than that of the Egyptian monk; but he was conscious of the dangers of eye contacts in church, of which he himself had experience as a student at Carthage[56] and now bitterly deplored; but in those days he had not been dedicated to continence.

A similar provision covers other sins, which are to be handled "with love of the persons and hatred of the offenses" (4.10), and specifically the case of a monk who has received "letters or little gifts from a woman secretly" (4.11). Such an incident would, in itself, bring scandal upon a religious house;[57] but Augustine is also concerned with the question of gifts given by parents to their offspring now in the monastery, laying it down that any such present must be handed over to the superior to be put into the common stock for those who needed them (5.3). Similar regulations are to be found in the Benedictine *Rule* 54. The underlying consideration is clear: the monk has left his natural family and joined a new monastic family, in which the only distinction in material well-being is determined by individual need. Accordingly, however great may be the love of a monk's human parents, they cannot be allowed to make him materially privileged among his spiritual brethren. This would have been hard to accept in Roman society, in which the ties of blood were extremely strong; but it was one of the sacrifices which had to be made, both by the monk and by his loved ones. *If any man comes to me and does not hate his own father and mother and wife and children and brothers and sisters, yes, and even his own life, he cannot be my disciple* (Lk 14:26).

Augustine now turns once more to the question of the monk's clothing, which he has already discussed in *Rule* 4.1. His emphasis here is on the desirability of the individual's being ready to accept clothes which have been previously worn by another member of the community. To object to doing this shows a lack of humility, the virtue which Augustine supremely valued. He grudgingly allows concessions to be made to personal sensitivity but insists that no garment is to be retained by an individual for his exclusive, personal use, but that it must be put into the common store (5.1), However, he accepts that a need may arise to have a change of clothing or shoes at any time of the day and directs that the storekeepers should always be ready to make a change, if requested to do so (5.11).

Communal labor

The common use of clothing leads Augustine to a discussion of communal labor: "No one should work at anything for himself. All your work should be shared together with greater care and more ready eagerness than if you were doing things for yourself alone" (5.2). Augustine does not specify the character of the work, which is performed from the early morning until noon, and again after the main meal of the day, taken in the afternoon, when the monks are to work in the garden or perform similar tasks until lamp lighting (Vespers) (*Ordo* 3). It is apparently envisaged that some of the produce of the monastery should be offered for sale, since monks who are sent to market it are told not to do anything contrary to their instructions (*Ordo* 8).[58] To what extent these internal productions contributed to the economic viability of the monastery we do not know.

It has been said that monasticism made manual labor acceptable to the upper classes of medieval society, where freedom from the necessity to work on the land or in the shop was the social determinant. (In English, the word "gentleman" originally meant a man who could live off the produce of the land which he owned without himself laboring.[59]) Augustine, for his part, was determined that his monks should work with their hands as well as read books. About the year 400 he received a request from his friend and colleague, Aurelius, bishop of Carthage, to refute some monks at Carthage who declined to do manual labor but preferred to live on the gifts of the faithful, devoting themselves to prayer and disregarding Saint Paul's precept: *If any man will not work neither let him eat* (2 Thes 3:10), taking as their authority Christ's words: *Look at the birds of the air. They neither sow nor reap nor gather into barns and yet your heavenly father feeds them* (Mt 6: 26). This movement had started in the East, where its followers were known as Euchites— "men of prayer"[60]—and a pleasant story is told about a euchite monk who visited Abba Silvanus on Mount Sinai and, seeing the brethren working, counseled them *not to labor for the food that perishes* (Jn 6:27) but to choose the way of Mary (Lk 10: 42). Abba Silvanus ordered the visitor to be shown to a cell and left to pray. At the ninth hour—about 3 p.m.—the usual time for dinner, the euchite expected to be called to eat, but no one came. At last he left his cell and went to Silvanus to ask about dinner time, to be told that the brethren had already eaten. "You are a spiritual person and do not need food. We are earthly, and since we want to eat, we work with our hands. But you have chosen the good part, reading all day and not wanting to take earthly food." Humbled, the monk prostrated himself at Silvanus' feet, saying: "Forgive me, Abba," and the old man said: "I think that Mary always needs Martha, and by Martha's help, Mary is praised."[61] These are exactly Augustine's views. At the same time he did not object to monastic houses receiving gifts from the faithful, thereby approving a form of piety which was eventually to produce the rich religious houses of the later middle ages, where individual poverty often went hand-in-hand with corporate wealth.[62]

Augustine answered Aurelius' request with the treatise *De Opere Monachorum*—*The Work of Monks*—in which he first argued against the exegesis of the texts which the Euchites used to defend their position. He then turned to the practical aspect of the religious life, arguing—as he does in the *Rule for Men*—that if rich people, who enter religion and surrender all their property to the monastery, would also assist in manual labor, this would take away all excuses from those who, coming from a humble background to a condition better than that to which they had been accustomed, might be tempted to live like lords and avoid all physical exertion (see *Rule* 3.4: "All should not desire to receive the extra things which they see given to a few—such things are a concession, not an honor. Otherwise a detestable disorder would arise in the monastery, if the rich work there as hard as ever they can, while the poor, who have greater strength, become soft"). There is, however, a significant aside in *The Work of Monks* 25.33, where Augustine faces the issue: if the rich recruits who have benefitted the monastery from their abundant possessions are unwilling to perform manual labor, "who would dare to compel them (*quod quidem si nolint, quis audeat cogere*)?" and suggests that some other tasks may be found for them, which are less demanding physically, "so that not even these should eat their bread without earning it, since the food is community property." This passing remark indicates the degree to which the rich and powerful who have entered the monastery might retain their prestige and stand upon their dignity even if they had abandoned their material possessions. In human relations, a gap remains between the ideal and the reality.

Nevertheless, Augustine is insistent that physical work is part of the monk's vocation and that a good part of his day should be devoted to manual labor, carried out with a minimum of conversation (*Ordo* 9), before proceeding to three hours of reading before dinner (*Ordo* 3). Writing as bishop of Hippo, Augustine declared that he would

> much prefer to do some manual labor at certain hours each day, as is the custom in well-regulated monasteries, and to have other hours free for reading, prayer, or for the study of the sacred scriptures, than to endure the very confusing perplexities of the problems of others in regard to worldly concerns which must be eliminated by our judgments or curtailed by our action.[63]

As a bishop he had, on occasion, to act as a judge in secular matters, sometimes fasting, says Possidius, until dinner time at the ninth hour and sometimes even for the whole day,[64] so it may be believed that he meant what he said. However, his words emphasize his concern for manual labor as part of the life of a monastery. But more than this: work should be pursued not simply because it is in the rule, but from love of the brethren. "The more you are concerned about the common good rather than your own, the more progress you will know that you have made" (5.2).

Bodily Care

Care for the physical well-being of the individual, in sickness and health alike, is an index of the concern felt in a community for its members. Understandably, perhaps, Augustine's provisions were governed by an ascetic spirit, which had no use for fastidiousness. Thus he lays it down that the washing of clothes is to be undertaken at the discretion of the superior, "so that too great a desire for clean clothing may not cause interior uncleanness of mind" (5.4).[65] This might seem a moderate degree of self-denial, until one remembers the heat of North Africa in the summer months and the fact that Augustine and his brethren probably wore cloaks of linsey-woolsey, not linen,[66] like the monks of *The Rule of the Master* 81 at a later date, which, unless frequently washed, would give off a strong body odor. Nevertheless, although desiring to deny his monks the sensual pleasure of newly-washed garments, Augustine does not want to carry asceticism so far as to endanger their health. Monks may go to the public baths for reasons of health, and even if an individual does not want to go and his well-being demands it, the superior should command him to do so for his health's sake (5.5). Conversely, if a visit to the baths is judged inopportune and a monk asks for it, permission is to be withheld. The public baths of Roman cities resembled the modern Turkish baths, with heat and sweating followed by a cold plunge, and were deemed conducive to health. On the other hand, they were also believed to stimulate sexual appetite. Saint Jerome, as might be expected, did not believe that a virgin dedicated to religion should ever visit the baths:

> If she mortifies and enslaves her body by vigils and fasting, if she desires to quench the flame of lust and to check the hot desires of youth by a cold chastity, if she hastens to spoil her natural beauty by a deliberate squalor, why should she rouse a sleeping fire by the incentive of baths?[67]

Augustine was aware of this other aspect of bathing and of the possibility that a visit to the baths might give rise to, or be an excuse for, other less innocent activities,[68] and therefore laid it down that if monks were to go to the baths they should go in a party of two or three, their companions being not of their own choosing but of the superior's (5.7).

All this may seem narrow and trivial, the mark of a vanished age and the transformation of brotherly relationships into the petty disciplinary system of a school, but the foundation of Augustine's view of the treatment of the sick is expressed in a single sentence:

> Finally, if one of the servants of God has a hidden pain and reports it, he is to be believed without hesitation; but if it is uncertain whether what he asks will cure his pain, the doctor should be consulted. (5.6)

When there is a question of possible real illness, the patient is to be believed without question. Furthermore, a designated individual is to act as the infirmarian or community nurse, with authority to draw from the storeroom whatever he considers to be necessary for the patient's welfare (5.8). We have already seen that, in treatment during illness and convalescence, no distinction is to be made between those who came into the monastery from a life of poverty and those who enjoyed a high standard of living. Any distinction made thereafter will be determined by the speed of recovery, which Augustine believes will be more rapid in the case of those who have been hardened by a life of poverty (3.5).

If the care of the sick is to be reckoned as an indication of the moral stature of a religious community, the Augustinian house comes out well, though it should be recognized that both *The Rule of the Master,* 69-70, and the Benedictine *Rule,* 36, also make careful provision for those taken ill. *The Rule of the Master,* after an initial scepticism designed to deter possible malingering, encourages the brethren to visit their sick fellows and so fulfill Christ's saying: *I was sick and you visited me* (Mt 25:36). The Benedictine *Rule* quotes Matthew 25:36 while at the same time reminding the sick not to burden their brethren with unnecessary demands. Sickness, in fact, provides an opportunity for the exercise of charity by both the sick and those who minister to them.

Grumbling

Augustine adds that those who are responsible for the storeroom, the wardrobe, and the library of the monastery should serve the brethren without murmuring (5.9), thus making specific a general principle laid down in *Regulations for a Monastery* 5: "Let no one grumble in whatever he has to do, lest he incur the judgment of the grumblers [in the wilderness]."

The sentiment is obvious—*God loves a cheerful giver* (2 Co 9:7) —and is elaborated in *The Rule of the Master* 7.71-72:

> The disciple obeys with ill will if he reproaches not only us verbally but God inwardly about what he does in a bad mood. And even though he does what he was commanded, still it will not be acceptable to God, who sees that he is murmuring in his heart.

This is copied by Saint Benedict (5.17-18). The commandment against grumbling is an obvious one. Few practices are more calculated to poison the atmosphere of a community than discontent, either concealed or openly expressed, and this will be particularly true of a community associated by common friendship. Ideally, the bonds of friendship will prevent grumbling, but in an imperfect world friendship may need to be reinforced by exhortation or even by direct command. Augustine recognized this, inserting a clause specifically against grumbling into the *Ordo* (5).

Besides grumbling, however, it is possible to have disagreement in the community, which may turn into open quarreling which, Augustine notes (6.1) can, if not brought to a speedy reconciliation, grow into hatred, and *anyone who hates his brother is a murderer* (1 Jn 3:15). For this reason Augustine urges that quarrels be resolved as soon as possible by mutual apologies and forgiveness by the parties involved. He considers that it is better for an individual to be hot-tempered and so be quickly moved to anger and then be quick to ask forgiveness than to be slow to wrath and then to nourish resentment and refuse to ask for pardon. Indeed, he says bluntly that anyone who is never willing to ask pardon or who does not ask for it sincerely ought not to be in a monastery: "You should take care, then, not to use harsh words; but if they should have escaped from your mouth, then do not be ashamed to let the mouth which caused the wound provide the cure" (6. 2).[69]

It is in the context of quarreling that Augustine's Letter 211, called by Verheijen the *Obiurgatio—Rebuke for Quarreling Nuns*—needs to be considered, together with its predecessor, Letter 210, which has a similar theme. Letter 211 was long considered as both introducing and incorporating the *Regularis Informatio,* the feminine version of the *Rule.* Codicological study has raised doubts as to whether the *Rule for Women* was originally attached to the letter; it may be that it only became attached to it later, in the course of transcription. Whatever the textual history, there is no reason for not making use of the letter, and its predecessor, to illustrate Augustine's reactions to divisions within a community.

Letter 210 is addressed to a Mother Felicitas, to a Brother Rusticus (perhaps a presbyter and spiritual director), and to the sisters of a convent in which dissensions had arisen. There is no indication of the date and no information as to how the dissensions arose. What is clear is Augustine's anxiety that the quarrel should be healed as soon as possible, on the principle enunciated in the *Rule:* "Bring quarrels to an end as quickly as possible, lest anger grow into hatred—a straw into a plank—and produce a murderous heart" (6:1). In Letter 210 the effect of anger on the human heart is likened to the action of vinegar left in a metal pitcher, if it is allowed to remain (2). Disagreements must never be welcomed, though they can be of value if they arise from a loving rebuke or reveal the sincerity of the reprover's love. We have a moral duty, says Augustine, to rebuke an erring sister, and even if she argues and refuses to accept correction it may come about that, left to herself in solitude, in the presence of God, she will come to see the justice of the reprimand, amend her ways, and see that the reprover was motivated by love.

Letter 211, which has attracted far more attention from scholars because of its presumed connection with the *Rule for Women*, bears no address. It concerns an unnamed superior of a convent, who apparently had been second-in-command of the community under Augustine's sister, a widow who after her husband's death had entered religion; a presbyter, who was apparently Augustine's liaison officer with the convent; and the divided and rebellious community, some of whom wanted to change their superior (Letter 211, 4). In some way the presbyter was involved in the dispute, to his great embarrassment, since it was rumored that he had provided the inspiration for the demand for a new superior—an allegation which he vigorously denied, threatening to resign (Letter 211, 4). A request had been made to Augustine to visit the community in person, which he had refused, believing, he said, that it would only have added to the dissensions (Letter 211,1).

Whatever else this letter reveals, it shows the limitations both of Augustine's personal ability to deal with the disturbance, short of threatening to excommunicate the rebels, which he does not, and of the prestige and powers of the superior. On paper, as we have seen, these were considerable, and the religious were expected to submit out of holy obedience (7.1,4; *Ordo* 6). However, the Augustinian superior was not endowed with the absolute powers of the Egyptian abbot and, if we may judge from Letters 210 and 211 (which could conceivably refer to the same incident),[70] Augustine did not seek to endow him or her with an equivalent of abbatial authority. Consider the opening of Letter 211: Augustine has declined the request to visit the community personally because, he says, a visit would have forced him to punish severely any disturbance occurring in his presence, which would only have added to the community's troubles. This refusal may indicate diplomatic caution; but it left the superior and the priest without any visible support in what must have been a humiliating experience for both of them. Instead, Augustine wrote an emotional letter, reminding the nuns of their superior's career as a mother of the community and its flourishing state under her past and present leadership. If he had visited the convent in person, announced his unqualified support for the superior and the presbyter and exhorted the malcontents to return to unity, this would surely have been more effective than a letter, however well written. Perhaps

Augustine, like other men of the pen, overestimated the short-term power of the written word; but the old rhetorician ought to have remembered the effect of words spoken by a master of oratory.

It is possible that Letter 211 provides a clue to Augustine's personality which may, in turn, illuminate the mood of the *Rule:* in dealing with people Augustine may have lacked the dominating temperament which characterizes more forceful religious leaders like Saint Ambrose or Saint Bernard of Clairvaux: he was not at his best in a hostile confrontation. One can point, by way of illustration, to his failure to control his congregation at Hippo in 411, when his parishioners attempted to constrain him to ordain the visiting Roman senator Pinianus, in the hope that his wealth would come to the church of Hippo.[71] Augustine's showing on that occasion fell far short of what we would have expected in a Cyprian. His was an inspiring but not a masterful personality. He could, and did, attract admirers, but did not dominate, and this may help to explain the character of the *Rule:* the superior's authority ultimately rested upon the love and affection of his brethren. He might turn to the presbyter for support, and the presbyter might refer the matter to the bishop, but there could be no certainty of episcopal support. In Augustine's age canon law in North Africa was in its infancy,[72] and monasticism was still very much a matter of private concern, uncontrolled by general legislation. A lay movement, its control and clericalization in the course of the following centuries was not the least of the achievements of the episcopate. It seems clear, too, that Augustine, in theory and practice alike, regarded his monastery as a particular association and not a pattern for a widespread religious congregation. Significantly, he did not himself call *the Rule for Men* a rule

(*regula*) but a *libellus,* a memorandum or booklet, intended
to provide the community with a mirror in which individuals might view themselves and judge how far they had
progressed in a life dedicated to the love of God and of their
brethren (8.2).

Other Themes

Such is the *Rule for Men,* ascribed to Saint Augustine and
today generally accepted by modern scholars as his composition. It takes for granted an already-existing community
and its continuance. It makes no provision for any formal
admittance for new members or for the succession to the
current superior, as do the *Regula Magistri* and the Benedictine *Rule.* It provides no practical details of the diet of the
monks or of the clothing which they wore. We know from
the *Ordo* that wine was provided on Saturdays and Sundays
for those who wanted it, which would imply that some of
the community were abstainers; otherwise we are told
nothing about the sort of food provided, though it may be
assumed that for healthy members it would have been vegetarian. We are told that there was reading at mealtimes.
Time was set apart for personal reading each day, but all
that we know about the library—which was presumably a
large one, formed from the books contributed by well-off
recruits and being continually augmented by Augustine's
own compositions—is that books were issued daily at a
definite time, and not at the whim of the borrower. The
nature of what was to be read was not specified. Regular
prayer and regular manual labor are taken for granted.

A feature of the *Rule* which may seem curious is the
absence, apart from the warning against eye contacts with

women, of any discussion of sexual problems of the celibate. Here we find a marked contrast not only to the writings inspired by the Egyptian desert, where sexual
temptation was routinely discussed, but also to *The Rule of
the Master,* which deals at some length with topics like the
treatment of lustful thoughts and whether a brother who
has suffered nocturnal pollution may receive communion.
One cannot suppose that Augustine was unaware of such
problems. When he wrote the *Soliloquies,* soon after his
conversion, he began by saying that he had decided to
renounce all relations with women, "for I feel that nothing
so depresses the manly intelligence than the caresses of a
woman. . . . I am completely free from desires of this kind
and I recall them with horror and disdain" (1.10.17), only
to admit the next day how different his thought and fanta-
sies had been the previous night (1.14.25). Some ten years
later, in the *Confessions,* he admitted that sexual fantasy
remained powerful: "So strongly does the illusory image in
my mind affect my body that these unreal figments influence me in sleep in a way that the reality could never do
while I am awake" (10.30.41). Since these experiences
would not have been peculiar to Augustine, and since the
degree of sinfulness attaching to them was to continue to
exercise the minds of later moral theologians,[73] and since he·
had no hesitation in discussing sexuality in other writings of
his, often at wearisome length, it seems strange that he did
not address sexual problems in the *Rule,* under the general
theme of chastity. It may be that he considered this as a
matter for private conferences rather than for publication
in writing. More probably, however, in the present writer's
opinion, the absence is due to the fact that the *Rule for Men*
is to be seen not as an amplification of *Regulations for a
Monastery* but rather as a collection of reflections upon it,[74]

in no way comprehensive in scope, rather haphazardly arranged, and intended for domestic use and not for export, although it could, and did, provide inspiration for other religious houses. This would explain why the *Rule* is not listed in the *Revisions*—Augustine did not regard it as being a publication, but as a set of "house rules" for a particular community. For himself, he lived and died a monk and turned his episcopal household into a monastery; but he did not set out to found a religious order.

Augustinian Monasticism: Epilogue

What are the distinguishing marks of Augustinian monasticism? First and foremost is the notion of a religious community brought together by a friendship founded upon a common love of God and not by submission to a human teacher. This represented a departure from the abbatial tradition of Egypt, which had been, and remains, the mark of what may be called classic monasticism. Its form may be seen as deriving from Augustine's temperament and from the circumstances of his career. Initially his friends had been fellow intellectuals like Alypius and Evodius. During his period as presbyter and bishop of Hippo, many recruits to the monastery apparently came from the lower, or even the servile, ranks of society, yet they had to be accepted, "for many of that class have been truly great and worthy of imitation" (*The Work of Monks* 22.25), and the only distinction among members of the community was to be based on physical stamina: "The less God's servants need, the more fitting it is. . . . It is better to need less than to have more" (*Rule* 7.3).

As a result, there is in Augustine's monasticism what might be called a democratic element.[75] The term must not be exaggerated—the notions of Augustine's age were very different from our own—but there is in friendship an inevitably egalitarian quality if it is to be called friendship at all. Love does not, in itself, make for equality; but to be friends, individuals need to find some common level which makes them equal, even if it does not extend to all their relationships. The Augustinian superior is, inevitably, a man under authority in his dealings with the brethren, but "he should consider himself lucky[76] not in having power over you but in being able to care for you with love" (7.3).

For Augustine, as for other monastic theologians, the life of the monk is made up of prayer, study, and physical labor. Prayer inevitably includes the daily office (*Ordo* 2; *Rule* 2.1), but Augustine takes it for granted that the individual will pray privately and for that reason lays it down that the oratory is not to be used for any purpose other than for prayer, so that a monk will be able to pray outside the fixed hours of community services if he has time (2. 2). Augustine regards prayer as being fundamentally a matter of intention rather than of words. The injunction of 1 Thes 5:17, *Pray without ceasing*, is both a challenge and a puzzle to the devout Christian. In Eastern Christendom the solution to the command to pray without ceasing is found in the devotion of the famous Jesus Prayer, a repetition, conscious or unconscious, of the invocation "Lord Jesus Christ, have mercy upon me a sinner!" which words, being continually repeated, eventually became an automatic mental activity.[77] For Augustine the essence of prayer is the desire for God, a fixing of our attention upon him, lifting our thoughts from the earth.

Lift up your hearts to heaven! You ask: "How can I do it? What ropes are needed? What machinery, what ladders?" The steps are your affections, your will is the way. You ascend by loving, by neglect you descend. If you love God you are in heaven while standing upon the earth, for the heart is not raised as the body is raised. When the body is raised it changes its place: when the heart is raised it changes its desire.[78]

Like other patristic teachers, Augustine regards the Lord's Prayer as the perfect example. He emphasizes that in praying it is not enough simply to recite the words: "We must ourselves pray in the words we utter. When you pray to God in *psalms and hymns,* meditate in the heart on what is expressed with the voice" (2.3). Again he says, with regard to one of the psalms: "If the psalm is praying, pray yourselves; if it is groaning, you groan; if it is happy, rejoice; if it is crying out in hope, you hope as well; if it expresses fear, be afraid. Everything written here is like a mirror held up to us" (*Exposition of Psalm* 30, exp. 4.1). The Christian must identify himself with the words of the prayers which he utters and not simply repeat a formula.

That Augustinian monasticism will have an intellectual quality may be taken for granted. The *Ordo* directs that some three hours a day should be devoted to reading *Ordo* 3. Augustine, while approving the reception of recruits of lower-class or servile origins, says nothing about illiterate monks in the monastery. It can only be conjectured that those unable to read were given instruction.

Manual labor as part of the monastic profession is not only taken for granted in the *Ordo* and in the *Rule* but forcefully defended in *The Work of Monks.* In this, Augustine followed long-established tradition, and the only thing to be remarked is the vehemence with which he asserted its necessity against the Euchites.

In a wider spiritual context one may note the absence from the *Rule* of that sense of sin and fear of damnation which appears so frequently in the *Sayings of the Desert Fathers*[79] and of the fund of stories about demons, who haunted the desert wastes.[80] Certainly Augustine believed in demons and in their hostility to the human race. In *The City of God* 22.8, he tells of a man named Hesperius, the owner of an estate in the district of Fussala, near Hippo, whose animals and slaves suffered from the attacks of evil spirits, from which they were delivered only when one of Augustine's clergy visited the farm and celebrated the eucharist, praying that the mischief might cease. The exorcism was immediately effective. In the *Rule,* however, Augustine says nothing about demonic temptations of the mind. Considering his theological concern with human sin, one might have expected frequent reminders, but this is not the case and it is possible to regard the *Rule* as being, under divine grace, an optimistic document. The brethren are not expected to indicate a sense of personal sinfulness by any external indication of humility. Nowhere is it said that the monk should declare aloud that he is lower and more worthless than anyone else, "a worm, not a man, the scorn of men and despised by the people," as in *The Rule of the Master* 10.68-69, and in the Benedictine *Rule* 7.52, nor, still less, that he should display himself "with head always bowed, his gaze fixed on the ground, at all times conscious that he is guilty because of his sins, imagining that he is already appearing at the fearful judgement" (*Rule of the Master* 10.83-84; Benedictine *Rule* 7.62-66). Rather, Augustine's particular concern is that the monk should not make himself conspicuous: "In walking, in standing, and in all your movements, nothing should be done that might cause offense to anyone who sees you; everything should be in keeping with your holy state" (4.3). No moral theologian sets a higher value than Augustine on humility and the danger of pride, "for every other vice prompts people to do evil deeds; but pride lies in ambush even for good deeds in order to destroy them" (1.7); but he does not demand any outward display of humility. What he does regard as a test of true humility is a readiness to wear clothes which another person has worn earlier. "If . . . someone . . . considers that it is beneath his dignity to wear what another brother has worn, this shows how far you are lacking in holiness in the holy interior clothing of your heart, since you dispute about the clothing of the body" (5.1). This saying would have been approved in frugal families down through the ages, where it would be customary to hand on clothing from an older child to a younger,[81] but it also indicates Augustine's practical understanding of the demands of humility in a Christian community united by friendship. The monks are not *slaves under the law but . . . free persons established in grace* (Rom 6:14,16) (8.1).[82] For Augustine there can never be absolute freedom in a created being, which is dependent on God for its existence, but under divine grace we are made free to submit ourselves to God's will, so that we come to share in His freedom by that participation in him which is called deification.[83] It is possible to understand the alarmed reactions of the monks of Hadrumetum to the stringent anti-Pelagianism of Augustine's later years if their understanding of his theology had originally been shaped by the monastic spirit of the *Rule*.[84]

If, therefore, we understand spirituality as "an orientation of the mind and will to God, expressed in an individual's life and teaching," we will find it in Augustine's *Rule* in the notion of having *"one soul and one heart* centered on God" (1.2)—"Before all else, dearest brothers, let God be loved and then your neighbor" (*Ordo* 1), with that love being expressed in a common life, with no exaggerated display of piety, within the monastery or without. The monk offers himself to God entirely, but without ostentation.[85] There is a moderation in Augustine's outward devotion which conceals the conviction within:

> The trivial round, the common task
> Will furnish all we ought to ask,
> Room to deny ourselves, a road
> To bring us daily nearer God.

The *Rule*, of course, only represents one aspect, an outward and visible aspect, of Augustine's spirituality. He does not treat of the heights of contemplation, nor of Christian perfection, still less of the mysteries of divine providence and predestination. While the call of God is absolute, the monk does not need to pursue extreme asceticism to aspire to the kingdom of heaven. Augustine would have agreed with Abba Pambo when he declared: "We have not been taught to kill our bodies but to kill our passions."[86] Christians are commanded to love God with all their heart and soul and to love their neighbor as themselves. This commandment is at the heart of Augustinian monasticism.

Notes

1. *Confessions* 4.4.7-12.
2. *Confessions* 6.14.24
3. Augustine calls Monica "our mother," perhaps to suggest that she was not only the physical mother of himself and Navigius but spiritually the mother of the whole party.
4. See Lawless, *Augustine of Hippo and his Monastic Rule* 45-58.
5. See Peter Brown, *Augustine of Hippo* 132-137.
6. Sermon 355. 2: "I whom by God's grace you see before you as your bishop came to this city as a young man; many of you know that. I was looking for a place to establish a monastery and live there with my brothers." Trans. Hill, *Sermons* III/10, 166.
7. Possidius, *Life of Augustine* 31.6; see *Sermon* 355. 2. 6.
8. *Confessions* 8.6.14-15.
9. *Ibid.*, 8.5.12.
10. *Ibid.*, 8.6.15.
11. The Benedictine editors dated it to about 423 and were followed by J. H. Baxter in his edition in the Loeb series. However, the emendation by the Benedictines themselves of the reading *de deo natis* to *Donatistas* in paragraph 4 suggests a date after the Conference of Carthage, in 411 or 412. See Lawless, *op. cit.* 153: "Augustine's contrast between schism in the community of nuns and his rejoicing over unity with the Donatists hardly allows an interval of more than ten years after the event."
12. It may be that Letters 210 and 211 refer to the same incident.
13. See *Constitutiones Ordinis Fratrum S. Augustini* (Rome, 1968) and the translation by Robert P. Russell, *The Rule of Our Holy Father Augustine* (Villanova, Penn.: Province of Saint Thomas of Villanova, 1976).
14. See the comment of Lawless, *op. cit.* 169: "There is nothing in this monastic code which would contradict Augustine's authorship."
15. Jerome, Letter 22.34.
16. In his own legislation Augustine replaced the title of dean (*decanus*) with that of superior (*praepositus*).
17. See Sermon 355. 2, quoted above, note 5.
18. See Letter Divjak, 20* 5. Trans. by Robert B. Eno, *Saint Augustine. Letters 1*-29** (The Fathers of the Church 81) (Washington, D.C. : The Catholic University of America Press, 1989) 136.

19. We are not told whether the punishment was formally inflicted or administered on the spot by the *praepositus*.

20. Horace, *Ep*. 2.1.70-71; Ausonius, *Ad nepotem Ausonium*. 24-34.

21. See *Confessions* I, 9, 14.

22. *City of God* 22.2.

23. Benedictine *Rule* 45.3.

24. Eve D'Ambra, *Art and Identity in the Roman World* (London: Calman and King 1998) 135, fig. 94, draws attention to a statue of a house-slave from the House of the Ephebe at Pompeii (first century A.D.), which is a demeaning caricature. It should be added that some former owners treated their freedmen with a generosity which enabled them to leave impressive funeral monuments, designed to display their improved status and affluence (D'Ambra, *op. cit.*, 45ff.).

25. Saint John Chrysostom found it necessary, on occasion, to exhort the aristocratic Christian ladies of his congregation not to whip their maids brutally for trivial faults.

26. *The Sayings of the Desert Fathers: The Alphabetical Collection*, trans. by Benedicta Ward (Cistercian Studies Series No 59) (Kalamazoo, Mich.: Cistercian Publications, revised ed. 1984) 208-210.

27. See *City of God* 5, 26.

28. See Luc Verheijen, *Saint Augustine's Monasticism in the Light of Acts 4:32 -35.* (The Saint Augustine Lecture 1975) (Villanova University Press, l979).

29. *Ibid.*, 97. Other authors call it a "dynamic" process.

30. It is frequently cited by both Pachomius and John Cassian. See Adalbert de Vogüé, *The Rule of the Master*, trans. by Luke Eberle (Kalamazoo, Mich.: Cistercian Publications, 1977) 71, note 120; and *idem, Théologie de la vie monastique* (Paris: Aubier, 1961) 67-71, 215, to which de Vogüé refers.

31. de Vogüé, *op. cit.* 61, 62. This conception of the monastery as a school continued to be influential in the thought of St. Bernard in the twelfth century. See Etienne Gilson, *The Mystical Theology of St. Bernard*, trans. by A.H.C. Downes (London, 1940), chapter III: *Schola Caritatis*, 60-84.

32. *Ibid.* 62.

33. It should be remembered that, for a Roman, the word "father" had implications of authority which have disappeared today in most industrialized societies.

34. "The oldest surviving order of prayer in Western monasticism" (Zumkeller, *Augustine's Rule* 56).

35. See *Soliloquies* 1.1.2-6.

36. See Augustine, Letter 130.9.18.

37. *Ibid*. 10.20. Translation by G. Bonnero. See van Bavel, *op. cit.* 63; Zumkeller, *Augustine's Rule* 60-63; Agatha Mary, *op. cit.* 97-99.

38. See the admirable study by Thomas Hand, *Augustine on Prayer,* new ed. (New York: Catholic Book Publishing Co. 1986) 102-24.

39. *Ibid*. 67-77.

40. See van Bavel, *op. cit.* 62; see Zumkeller, *op. cit.* 60.

41. See Augustine, Letter 55.18.34. See Zumkeller, *op. cit.* 59.

42. See *Confessions* 9.6.14.

43. *Confessions* 10.33.49.

44. See van Bavel, *op. cit.* 66: "It is remarkable how few severe ascetical elements are to be found in the *Rule.*"

45. See *Teaching Christianity* 1.4.4

46. See G. Bonner, "Augustine's Thoughts on This World and Hope for the Next," *The Princeton Seminary Bulletin,* Supplementary Issue No. 3 (1994) 85-103.

47. Presumably the monastic library was distinct from the episcopal library, for which Augustine made provision before his death (Possidius, *Life of Augustine* 31.6).

48. Possidius, *op. cit.* 22.2.

49. *Ibid*. 22.6-7.

50. *The Work of Monks* 22.25.

51. See Augustine, Sermon 356.13. See Agatha Mary, *op. cit.* 146, quoting Paulinus of Nola, Letter 2. She notes (p. 147) that Peter Salway, *Roman Britain* (Oxford: Clarendon Press, 1981) 655, has likened the *birrus* to a modern duffle-coat; but this conjecture is not decisive.

52. Benedictine *Rule* 55.7-8: "Monks must not complain about the color or coarseness of all these articles, but use what is available in the vicinity at a reasonable cost. However, the abbot ought to be concerned about the measurements of those garments, that they not be too short but fitted to the wearers."

53. *The Rule of the Master* 81.15-16.

54. Jerome, Letter 52. 9: "Vestes pullas aeque vita ut candidas; ornatus et sordes pari modo fugiendae, quia alterum delicias, alterum gloriam redolet."

55. *Sayings of the Fathers* 4. 62. Trans. by Owen Chadwick, *Western Asceticism* (Philadelphia: The Westminster Press, 1958) 58. This is only one among many examples of an exaggerated fear of the corrupting effect of dealings with women.

56. See *Confessions* 3.3.5.

57. See van Bavel, *op. cit.* 85.

58. See Benedictine *Rule* 57.4-6.

59. See Peter Laslett, *The World We Have Lost* (London: University Paperbacks, 1965) 29: . " . . . the primary characteristic of the gentleman was that he never worked with his hands on necessary, as opposed to leisurely, activities." See also p. 34.

60. See K. T. Ware, " 'Pray without ceasing' : The Ideal of Continual Prayer in Eastern Monasticism," *Eastern Churches Review* 2 (1969) 253-261.

61. Chadwick, *op. cit.* 10.69 pp. 119-120; see 12.9, pp. 142-143.

62. *The Work of Monks* 16.17: "Because of the occupations of the servants of God and the physical infirmities which can never be wholly eliminated, the apostle not only permitted the faithful to supply the needs of preachers but he recommended the practice most earnestly." See Verheijen, *Saint Augustine's Monasticism in the Light of Acts 32:32-35,* 18-19. 53.

63. *The Work of Monks* 29.37.

64. Possidius, *Life of Augustine* 19, 2-3.

65. See Jerome, Letter 12. 7: "If you wish to be, and not merely seem, a monk, have regard not for your property—you began your vows by renouncing it—but for your soul. Let a squalid garb be evidence of a clean heart; let a coarse tunic prove that you despise the world, provided only that you do not pride yourself on such things nor let your dress and language be at variance."

66. "Linsey-woolsey is a coarse cloth made of linen and wool, or cotton and wool, and was no doubt the traditional mantle of monks" (de Vogüé, *The Rule of the Master,* 245, n. 4).

67. Jerome, Letter 107.11; see Letter 125.7 to Rusticus: "Avoid hot baths: your aim is to quench the heat of the body by the help of chilling fasts."

68. Zumkeller, *The Rule of Saint Augustine* 98, says that the baths were "places of lechery," basing this statement on Augustine, *The Instruction of Beginners* 16.25, where he speaks of the *prurigo thermarum*— "the itch of the hot baths." While the baths did not always have a good reputation among Christian moralists, Augustine would seem here, like Jerome, n. 63 above, to be thinking of the effect upon the individual bather.

69. See Agatha Mary, *op. cit.* 272ff.

70. One could imagine that Letter 210 was a covering letter to 211, the latter being an episcopal directive designed to be read to the whole community.

71. See Augustine, Letters 125 and 126.

72. See Charles Munier, *Vie conciliaire et collections canoniques en Occident IVe—XIIe siècles* (London: Variorum Reprints, 1987); J.E. Merdinger, *Rome and the African Church in the Time of Augustine* (New Haven: Yale University Press, 1997).

73. See, for example, the letter of Augustine of Canterbury to Pope Gregory I in Bede, *Ecclesiastical History* 1.27, q.9.

74. See Agatha Mary, *op. cit.* 343: "Augustine's precepts do not provide a set of instructions which, if followed, would produce the model that was in his, the designer's, mind. They were offered to the monks of Hippo as providing general principles which do not have the force of law but describe likely circumstances in which it is possible for God's grace to have free play. The *Rule* is not a code of conduct to be accepted and acted upon but an instrument for measuring human stature." Compare the discussion of the Benedictine *Rule* by David Knowles, *From Pachomius to Ignatius. The Constitutional History of the Religious Orders* (The Sarum Lectures 1964-1965) (Oxford: Clarendon Press, 1966) 72-6.

75. See van Bavel, *op. cit.* 104: "It is . . . possible to detect in the democratic mould of Augustine's *Rule* . . . a kind of protest against Roman society, with its strongly juridical character and sharply demarcated power structures."

76. "Lucky" is the rendering of *felix*, chosen because, while an emperor may be "happy because successful . . . *felix* applied to an ordinary man indicates a situation which is not based on true merits or true facts. There is a distortion here which is brought out in the English word lucky (in itself a somewhat cheap word)" (Agatha Mary, *op. cit.* 66). Nevertheless, *felix* can also on occasion be rendered by "fortunate" or "blessed." Thus Virgil, speaking of Epicurus, says:

> Felix qui potuit rerum cognoscere causas
> atque metus omnes et inexorabile fatum
> subiecit pedibus, strepitumque Acherontis avari!
> fortunatus et ille, deos qui novit agrestes . . . .
> (*Georgics* II, 490-493)
> Blessed is he whose mind had power to probe
> The causes of things and trample underfoot
> All terrors and inexorable fate
> And the clamor of devouring Acheron.
> But happy too is he who knows the gods

Of the countryside . . . .
(Trans. by L. P. Wilkinson)

Epicurus was regarded by his disciples rather as a devout believer in the theory of evolution might regard Charles Darwin (see Lucretius, *De Rerum Natura*, I, 62-79) and Virgil here calls him *felix*; but he calls the countryman *fortunatus*, and "fortunate," unlike luck, is not a cheap word. Perhaps one might say that, while the superior is *lucky* in having authority, he is *happy* in being able to care for his fellows with love.

77. See Antoine Guillement, "The Jesus Prayer among the monks of Egypt," *Eastern Churches Review* 6 (1974) 66-71. The famous Russian spiritual classic, *The Way of the Pilgrim* (trans. by R. M. French, London: SPCK, new ed. 1954), is concerned with this devotion. Interestingly, the first exegesis of *Pray without ceasing* which the anonymous pilgrim heard was: "Ceaseless interior prayer is a continual yearning of the human Spirit for God" (p. 2). It left him unsatisfied.

78. Expositions of the Psalms 85.6. See Hand, *op. cit.* 92-93. Translation slightly modified.

79. See especially Book 3 of Chadwick, *The Sayings of the Fathers*, 43-48.

80. For references to demons in the Egyptian desert, see Benedicta Ward, *The Sayings of the Desert Fathers* (Cistercian Studies 59) (Kalamazoo, Mich.: Cistercian Publications, revised ed. 1984) 260 and Norman Russell and Benedicta Ward, *The Lives of the Desert Fathers* (Cistercian Studies 34) (Oxford/Kalamazoo, Mich.: Cistercian Publications, 1981) 176. For Pachomius' attitude, see Philip Rousseau, *Pachomius. The Making of a Community in Fourth-Century Egypt* (Berkeley: University of California Press, 1985) 134-141, who shows that while Pachomius believed in demons, like everybody else, his treatment of demonology was a subtle one: "Like the other famous Egyptian ascetics, he believed that he and his colleagues were witnesses to a cosmic conflict between God and the spirits of evil, but it was a conflict for the most part quite independent of their own states of soul" (p. 139). Both the *Rule of the Master* and the Benedictine *Rule* are restrained in their treatment of demons. In the Augustinian *Rule* they are simply not mentioned. It was not that Augustine denied their existence. He discusses them at length in *The City of God* and other writings and wrote *The Divination of Demons* specifically to discuss some of their extraordinary powers. See R. H. Barrow, *Introduction to Saint Augustine, The City of God* (London: Faber and Faber, Ltd.,

1950) 208-218; Inez Mary Bogan, *Saint Augustine: The Retractations* (The Fathers of the Church 60) Washington, D. C.: The Catholic University of America Press, 1968), 180-183; and *Augustine through the Ages*, art. "Demons," pp. 266-268. Augustine's demons, coming from Neoplatonist philosophy, are of a higher social order than their Egyptian counterparts. Like Pachomius, Augustine believed in a cosmic conflict between God and the demons but, again like Pachomius, he saw it as a conflict for the most part independent of states of soul.

81. See Agatha Mary, *op. cit.* 246: "In a family one is sometimes glad to have the use of something that belongs to another member, *provided that there is no obligation to do so*" (italics supplied).

82. *Ibid.* 334-342.

83. *Ibid.* 108-110.

84. Columba Stewart, *Cassian the Monk* (New York/Oxford: Oxford University Press, 1998), notes that "in terms of the *practice* of the Christian life, Augustine and Cassian may scarcely have differed" (p. 19). Cassian's concern was that the Augustinian doctrine of pre-destination "effectively excluded human responsibility from the process of salvation" (*ibid.*). For the Hadrumetum affair, see Rebecca Harden Weaver, *Divine Grace and Human Agency: A Study of the Semi-Pelagian Controversy* (Patristic Monographs 15) (Macon, Georgia: Macon University Press, 1986) 1-35.

85. Zumkeller, *Augustine's Rule* 95: "In these sentences of the *Rule* Augustine shows us a sure way to Christian perfection. No extraordinary feats are required, but only a simple fidelity in everyday life. Nor are difficult works of penance demanded, but only a love that serves continuously."

86. Benedicta Ward, *The Sayings of the Desert Fathers* 193, Poemen 184. Augustine would also agree with Poemen: "There are three things which I am not able to do without: food, clothing and sleep; but I can restrict them to some extent" (Poemen 185). He would not, however, have echoed Poemen's declaration: "Wine is not for monks," any more than did the Master, who makes generous provision (27), or Saint Benedict, who is more grudging (40).

III

The *Ordo Monasterii*

1. Before all else, dearest brothers, let God be loved and then your neighbor, because these are the chief commandments which have been given us.

2. We now set down how we ought to pray and recite the psalms. At morning prayer let three psalms be said: the sixty-second, the fifth, and the eighty-ninth.[1] At the third hour let one psalm first be said responsorially, then two antiphons,[2] a reading, and then the closing prayer. Let prayers be said in a similar fashion at the sixth and ninth hours. At lamplighting (*lucernarium*) a responsorial psalm, four antiphons, another responsorial psalm, a reading, and then the closing prayer. And at a suitable time after lamplighting, once all [the congregation] have been seated, there are to be readings, and afterwards the customary psalms before sleeping.[3] Now for the night prayers: in the month[4] of November, December, January and February, twelve antiphons, six psalms, and three readings. In March, April, September and October, ten antiphons, five psalms, and three readings. In May, June, July and August, eight antiphons, four psalms, and two readings.

3. [The monks] are to work from early morning to the sixth hour and then let them have time for reading from the

sixth hour to the ninth. At the ninth hour they are to hand back their books, and after they have eaten let them do some work in the garden or wherever it may be necessary until the time for lamplighting.

4. No one should claim anything as his own (Acts 4:32), whether in clothing or in anything else, since we choose to lead a life on the apostolic pattern.

5. Let no one grumble at whatever he has to do, lest he incur the judgement inflicted on grumblers.[5]

6. Let them obey faithfully. Let them honor their [spiritual] father next to God and submit to their superior *as becomes saints* (Eph 5:3).

7. Let them keep silence when they sit at table and listen to the reading. If anything is needed, their superior should take care of it. On Saturdays and Sundays, wine is to be provided for those who wish to have it, in accordance with the regulations.

8. If it is necessary for someone to be sent out from the monastery on some essential business, a pair should go together. No one is to eat or drink outside the monastery without permission, for such behavior does not accord with monastic discipline. If any brothers are sent to sell the produce of the monastery, let them take good care to do nothing contrary to their instructions, knowing that this would move God to anger against his servants. Again, if they buy anything needed by the monastery, let them act carefully and faithfully, as becomes the servants of God.

9. Let there be no idle talk among them. From break of day they are to sit at their various tasks, and after the prayers of the third hour let them go to work in similar fashion. They should not stand about telling stories (*fabulas contextant*) unless it concerns something useful to the soul.

Sitting at their tasks they are to keep silence unless by chance the needs of their work require someone to speak.

10. If anyone does not strive to carry out these things with all his strength, aided by the Lord's mercy, but stubbornly refuses to respect them and, after being warned once and again, does not amend his ways, let him know himself to be subject to the monastic discipline as may be fitting. If however his age shall be such [as to make it appropriate], he may even be whipped.[6]

11. By faithfully and prayerfully observing these things in Christ's name you, on the one hand, will make progress and we, on the other, will have no small joy in your salvation. Amen.

Notes

1. The *Ordo* here follows the numeration of the Greek Septuagint translation of the Psalms. The Hebrew numbers are 63, 5, and 91.
2. See above, p. 48, n. 27.
3. The "customary psalms before sleeping" are assumed to be known to the congregation. Are they the 4th, 90th and 133rd of the Benedictine *Rule*, 18? We do not know. Cassian, *Institutes* 4.19.2, speaks of "the psalms which those going to rest customarily sing." The compiler of the sixth-century *Rule of the Master* (37) also refers to three psalms which are to be said at compline, without indicating the number.
4. By a misprint, Verheijen's text gives *mena* (*Règle* I, 149 line 12). The correct reading is *mense*.
5. See Nm 14:1-37; Ps 94 (95): 7-11.
6. The only known example of such a punishment being inflicted in Augustine's community occurs in Letter 20*. 5 (Divjak), when a monk is said to have been whipped for talking to some nuns at an inappropriate time.

IV

The *Praeceptum*

1.1 You that are settled in the monastery, these are the things that we advise you to observe.

1.2 In the first place—and this is the very reason for your being gathered together in one—you should live in the *house in unity of spirit* (Ps 67:7[68:6]) and you should have *one soul and one heart* (Acts 4:32) centered on God.

1.3 And then, you should not call *anything your own, but you should have everything in common* (Acts 4:32). *Food and clothing* (1 Tm 6:8) should be allotted to you by your superior, not equally to all because you are not all equally strong, but to each one according to need. For thus you read in the Acts of the Apostles: *They had everything in common and distribution was made to each as any had need* (Acts 4:32:35).

1.4 At the moment of entering the monastery those who had any property in the world should gladly choose to have it become common property.

1.5 As regards those who had no possessions, they should not seek to have in the monastery things which they could not have had outside. Yet if, because of illness, they are in need, they should be given whatever is necessary, even though their poverty before entering was such that they could not even obtain necessities. They should not congratulate themselves on their good luck[1] in finding the sort of food and clothing that they could not find outside.

1.6   Nor should they give themselves airs because they find themselves in the company of people whom they would not have dared to approach outside; but they should *lift their heart on high* and not be seeking *earthly things* (Col 3:1-2) which are transitory. Otherwise, monasteries will become profitable to the rich and not to the poor, if the rich become humble there and the poor become puffed up.

1.7   On the other hand, those who were regarded in the world as persons of consequence should not look down on their brothers who have entered the religious community from humble circumstances. They should take pains to glory in the companionship of their poor brothers rather than in the rank of wealthy relatives. They should not boast if they have contributed anything to the common life from their own means, nor should they take more pride in their riches because they are sharing them in the monastery than they would if they were enjoying them in the world. For every other vice prompts people to do evil deeds; but pride lies in ambush even for good deeds in order to destroy them. What advantage is it *to scatter abroad and give to the poor* (Ps111(112):9; 2 Cor 9:9) and become poor oneself, if the wretched soul becomes prouder in despising riches than it was in possessing them?

1.8 Therefore you should all live *united in mind and heart* (Acts 4:32) and should in one another honor God,[2] whose temples you have become.[3]

2.1 *Persevere faithfully in prayers* (Col 4:2) at the appointed hours and times.

2.2 In the oratory, no one should do anything that conflicts with its purpose, implied by its name. Hence if those who happen to be free wish to pray there outside the fixed hours they should not be hindered by anyone who might think of doing something else there.

2.3 When you pray to God in *psalms and hymns* (Col 3:16), meditate in the heart on what is expressed with the voice.

2.4 And sing only what is set down for you to sing. But what is not written to be sung is not to be sung.

3.1 Discipline your flesh by fasting and abstinence from food and drink as far as your health allows. But when anyone cannot remain fasting, he should not take food apart from the midday meal (*prandium*) unless he is ill.

3.2 When you come to table, and until you rise, you should listen without interruption or discussion to what is read to you according to custom. Not only do your throats take food[4] but ears, too, hunger *for the word of God* (Amos 8:11).

3.3 If special treatment in the way of diet is given to those who are not strong as a result of their former way of life, others who are stronger because they have had a different manner of life must not be aggrieved or think it unfair. Nor should they think the former luckier in getting something that they themselves do not get. Rather, they should be thankful that they are strong enough to do what others cannot.

3.4 When those who have entered the monastery from a more luxurious way of life are given any food, clothing, bedding or covering that is not given to others who are stronger and more fortunate, these latter should consider how far the former have come down from their previous way of life in the world even though they cannot reach the simplicity of living which is possible for those who are stronger in body. All should not desire to receive the extra things which they see given to a few; such things are a concession, not an honor. Otherwise a detestable disorder would arise in the monastery, if the rich work there as hard as ever they can while the poor, who have greater strength, become soft.

3.5 As the sick need to eat little so that they do not become worse, so after illness they must certainly be given special care to help them get strong as soon as possible, even if they came from conditions of extreme poverty in the world. In fact, recent illness has made necessary for them what a former way of life has made necessary for the rich. But when they have recovered their strength they should resume their own more fortunate way of life, since the less God's servants need the more fitting it is. The state of luxury by which their need was relieved when they were ill should not hold them there when they are better. They should esteem themselves to be the richer who are stronger in enduring privations. It is better to need less than to have more.

4.1   Your clothing should not be conspicuous. You should try to please not by your clothes but by your behavior.

4.2   When you go out, walk together; and when you come to your destination, stay together.

4.3   In walking, in standing and in all your movements, nothing should be done that might cause offense to anyone who sees you; everything should be in keeping with your holy state.

4.4   Even if your gaze chances to fall on a woman you should not stare at her. There is no rule forbidding you to see women when you go out, but to attract or encourage their attention is wrong.[5] Nor is it only by touch and strong feelings that desire (*concupiscentia*) for women is aroused but also by the way of looking. You cannot claim to have pure minds if you have impure eyes, for an impure eye is the messenger of an impure heart. When impure hearts exchange messages by their glances, even though the tongue remains silent, and when through wrong desire they take pleasure in each other's ardor, then chastity takes flight from their behavior even though there has been no despoiling of the body.

4.5   Whoever lets his eye rest on a woman and takes pleasure in having hers rest on him should not imagine that he is not seen by others when he does so. He is bound to be noticed, and that by those he does not think have seen him. But even suppose he does conceal it and is seen by no human eye, what will he do about him who looks down from heaven and from whom nothing can be concealed?[6] Or are we to think that he does not see because his patience is as great as his wisdom? A man consecrated to holiness, then, should fear to displease him,[7] and then he will not want to please a woman in a wrong way. He should ponder the fact that God sees all things, and then he will not want to look at a woman in a wrong way. For it is fear of God that is commended to us in this connection when it is written: *He who stares fixedly is an abomination to the Lord* (Prv 27:20 LXX).

4.6 Therefore when you are together in church or elsewhere where women are also present, you should protect one another's modesty, for in this way *God who dwells within you* (1 Cor 3:16; 2 Cor 6:16) will protect you from within yourselves.

4.7 And if you should notice in any one of you such wanton eyes as I am speaking of, you should warn him at once so that what has begun may go no further and may be immediately corrected.

4.8 However, if after this warning you should see him do the same thing again, then or on another day, he who noticed it should report him as one who is hurt and in need of healing. First, however, it should be pointed out to a second or third person, so that he can be proved wrong by the *mouth of two or three witnesses* (Dt 19:15; Mt 18:16-17; 2 Cor 13:1) and can be restrained with whatever firmness seems suitable. Do not think that you are being a mischief-maker when you draw attention to this. On the contrary, you would be no more innocent yourselves if by silence you let your brothers be lost when by reporting the matter you could have corrected them. If your brother had a wound in his body which he wished to keep secret for fear of medical treatment, would it not be cruel to keep silent and compassionate to make it known? How much more, then, ought you to report him so that he does not suffer from a more terrible festering, that of the heart.

4.9   But before pointing it out to others by whom he could be proved in the wrong if he denies it, you should first report him to the superior if after a warning he has still neglected to reform. This is in the hope that he may be corrected more privately without anyone else needing to know about it. But if he denies it, then without his knowledge others are to be brought in so that he may be accused and proved wrong not by one witness but by *two or three, in the presence of all* (Dt 19:15; Mt18:16; 2 Cor 13:1; 1 Tm 5:19). If indeed he is actually proved guilty, he must accept such correction as will help him to amend, according to the judgement of the superior or of the presbyter who has power to give direction and make judgements. If he refuses to accept this, and yet does not withdraw of his own accord, he must be expelled from your fellowship.[8] And moreover this is not cruelty but compassion, lest he bring about the destruction of many by poisonous infection.

4.10   And what I have said about not staring unbecomingly should be applied carefully and faithfully to the discovery, warning, reporting, proving and punishing in the field of other sins too, and that with love of the persons and hatred of the offenses.

4.11   Someone may have gone so far wrong as to receive letters or little gifts secretly from a woman. Then, if he confesses of his own accord, he should be dealt with gently and prayer should be made for him. But if he is found out and proved guilty he should be corrected more strictly at the direction of the presbyter or the superior.

5.1 You should keep your clothes in one place under the care of one or two persons or as many as are needed to keep them shaken out and free from moths. Just as you are fed from a single storeroom so you should be clothed from a single wardrobe. As far as possible it should be a matter of indifference to you what is supplied for clothing according to the season— whether you receive what you left off or another garment which someone else has had before—so long as no one is denied what he needs.[9] But if quarrels and murmurings arise among you on this account and someone complains that he has received something that is not as good as what he had before, and he considers that it is beneath his dignity to wear what another brother has worn, this shows how far you are lacking in the holy interior clothing[10] of your heart, since you dispute about the clothing of the body. But even if concession is made to your weakness and you do receive what you left off, what you put aside must still be kept in one place under the common keepers.

5.2 So, then, no one should work at anything for himself. All your work should be shared together with greater care and more ready eagerness than if you were doing things for yourself alone. For when it is written of *love* that it *does not seek its own* (1 Cor 13:5), it means that it puts the common good before its own and not personal advantage before the common good. Thus the more you are concerned about the common good rather than your own, the more progress you will know that you have made. And thus the love that abides for ever[11] will reign in all matters of passing necessity.

5.3   It follows that, should anyone bring anything to his sons who are in the monastery or to others with whom he has a particular link, whatever the gift—be it clothing or any other article that is considered a necessity—it should not be received secretly but be given to the superior for him to put into the *common stock* so that it may be offered *to anyone who needs it* (Acts 4:32, 35).

5.4   Your clothes are to be washed at the discretion of the superior, either by yourselves or by the fullers, so that too great a desire for clean clothing may not cause interior uncleanness of mind.

5.5   Likewise, if someone's illness makes it necessary, bathing is not to be refused but on medical advice is to be done without murmuring. Even if he does not want it he must, at the command of the superior, do what has to be done for his health's sake. On the other hand, if he wants it and it is perhaps not expedient, he should not yield to his craving, for sometimes one thinks that what he likes will be good for him when in fact it is harmful.

5.6   Finally, if one of the servants of God has a hidden pain and reports it, he is to be believed without hesitation; but if it is uncertain whether what he asks for can cure his pain, the doctor should be consulted.

5.7   If you go to the baths, or wherever else it is necessary for you to go, there should not be fewer than two or three of you. A brother who has to go out should not choose his own companions but should go with those whom the superior appoints.

5.8 The care of the sick—whether they are convalescent or suffering from any bodily weakness even if there is no fever—should be entrusted to a particular person so that he may obtain from the storeroom what he sees each one needs.

5.9 Those who have charge of the storeroom, or the clothes, or the library, should serve their brothers without murmuring.

5.10 Books should be asked for at a definite time each day, and if anyone asks for them outside the time he should not be given them.

5.11 However, when there is need for clothes and shoes those who have charge of them should not delay to give them as required.

6.1 Do not have quarrels, or at least bring them to an end as quickly as possible, lest anger grow into hatred—a straw into a plank[12]—and produce a murderous heart. You have read the words: *Anyone who hates his brother is a murderer* (1 Jn 3:15).

6.2 If anyone hurts another by abuse or cursing, or by wild accusations, he should be careful to heal the wound he has made by apologizing as soon as possible; and the one who was hurt should himself be careful to forgive without further discussion. But if both have been hurtful they should forgive each other's offence, remembering the prayers which, because you repeat them so often, ought to be said with complete sincerity. Nevertheless, it is better to be one who is often tempted to give way to anger but quick to ask forgiveness of the person he admits he has injured than to be one who is more slowly roused to anger but finds more difficulty in asking pardon. Anyone who is never willing to ask pardon, or who does not ask it from his heart, is in the monastery without good reason even if he is not expelled. You should take care, then, not to use harsh words; but if they have escaped from your mouth, then do not be ashamed to let the mouth which caused the wound provide the cure.

6.3   But if the necessity of good order compels you to speak forcibly in order to put minors in their place,[13] even if you yourself feel that you have gone too far, it is not required of you to apologize to them. For it is their duty to defer to you, and your power to act should not be weakened by a display of excessive humility. All the same, you should ask pardon of the one who is Lord of all and who knows with what real concern even those whom you have reproved more severely than is just are loved by you. Moreover, even love among you must not be based on the standards of the world but on spiritual standards.

7.1   You should obey your superior as you would a father, with respect for his office, lest you offend God who is in him. This applies still more to the presbyter who has responsibility for you all.

7.2   It is chiefly the responsibility of the superior to see that all these instructions are complied with. If anything is not complied with he should not let it lapse through negligence but should take care that the matter is corrected and put right; thus he will refer to the presbyter who has the greater authority among you anything that exceeds his own province or powers.

7.3. All the same, he should consider himself lucky not in having power over you but in being able to care for you with love.[14] Before you he has to be at your head in honor; before God, he should be prostrate at your feet in fear. He should show himself to all around as a model of good works.[15] He should *restrain the restless, encourage the fainthearted, support the weak, be patient towards all* (1 Thes 5:14). He himself should keep these instructions gladly and so give them their due weight. And although both are necessary, he should seek rather your love than your fear, always bearing in mind the account he will have to render to God for you.

7.4 This is why, by being the more obedient, you show compassion not only to yourselves but also to him, for the higher the position held among you the greater the peril to him who holds it.

8.1 May the Lord grant that you observe all these things with love, as lovers of *spiritual beauty*,[16] spreading by your good life *the sweet odor of Christ* (2 Cor 2:15), not like *slaves under the law but as free persons established in grace* (Rom 6:14).

8.2 And so that you may be able to look at yourselves in this little book *as in a mirror*[17] it should be read to you once a week, lest you neglect anything through forgetfulness. When you find that you are doing the things that are written give thanks to the Lord, the giver of all good things. But when any one of you sees that he has failed in some way, he should be sorry for the past and be on his guard for the future, praying that his *sin may be forgiven* and that he may not be *led into temptation* (Mt 6:12-13; Lk 11:4).

Notes

1. See above, p. 103, n. 72.
2. See Rom 15:6.
3. See 2 Cor 6:16.
4. See Mt 4:4.
5. See Mt 5:28.
6. See Prv 24:18.
7. See *Ibid*.
8. See Mt 18:17.
9. See Acts 4:35.
10. See Ti 2:3. Some English versions have "reverent in behavior."
11. See 1 Cor 13:8.
12. See Mt 7:3-5.
13. Agatha Mary points out, *The Rule of St. Augustine* 275, that "it is impossible to be absolutely sure what was meant by the word *minores*, [although] it is certain that those referred to were in some sense in a disadvantageous position" because of youth, or spiritual inferiority or juniority. They could be children in the monastery, of whom the Benedictine *Rule* 70.4 lays down that they are to be disciplined by all adult members up to the age of fifteen.
14. See Lv 19:18; Rom 13:8-10; Gal 5:13.
15. See Ti 2:7.
16. Sir 44:6 Vulgate: *pulchritudinis studium habentes.*
17. See Jas 1:23-25.

V

Letter 210 (*Bonus est dominus*)

To the most beloved Mother Felicitas and to Brother Rusticus, and to the sisters who are with you, Augustine and those who are with me send greetings in the Lord.

1. *The Lord is good* (Lam 3:25) and his mercy is everywhere, which encourages us through your love [for him] in his heart.[1] How greatly he loves those who believe and hope in him and who love him and one another! And what he lays up for them in the future—he who *makes his sun rise on the good and the bad and his rain fall on the just and the unjust* (Mt 5:45)—he shows most chiefly in this, that he bestows many good things in this life on unbelievers, those without hope, and the hostile, against whom he threatens eternal fire with the devil[2] if they persist to the end in an evil will.

This is said briefly in order to make us reflect on it the more. For who is able to express the many benefits and unearned gifts which the godless enjoy in this life from him whom they scorn? Among these there is the great good that is proved by examples of intermingled calamities which, like a good physician, God mixes with sweetness in this present life, warning the wicked, if they care to listen, to *flee from the wrath to come* (Mt 3: 7) and, while they are *on the way* (Mt 5:25)—that is, in this life—to agree with the word of God, which they have made their *adversary* (Mt 5:25) by evil living. What then is not bestowed on people by the Lord God in his mercy, from whom even affliction is a kindness? For good fortune is God's gift that offers encouragement, misfortune is his gift that warns us. And if, as I said, he bestows these things, even on the wicked, what does he not prepare for those who wait for him?[3]

Rejoice, then, that you are of that number, being gathered together by his grace, *bearing with one another in love and seeking to preserve the unity of the Spirit in the bond of peace* (Eph 4:2-3). For what you are now going through for the sake of one another will not cease until the Lord has taken you away, and *death is swallowed up in victory,* that *God may be all in all* (1 Cor 15:54,28).

2. Dissensions ought never to be loved. But sometimes they are born of love or they put love to the test. For who can easily be found who wishes to be rebuked? And what about the wise one of whom it was said: *Rebuke a wise man and he will love you* (Prv 9:8)? Ought we not therefore to rebuke and correct a brother lest he go down to death in a false security? It can well be, and it often happens, that someone is offended when he is reproved and he resists and puts up a fight. Then later he may go over the matter in silence, where there is no one but God and himself; and he who does not fear to displease men because he has been rebuked does fear to displease God by not accepting correction. And from then on he will not do anything for which he can rightly be rebuked, and in the measure that he hates his sin he will love the brother who seemed to hate his sin.

But if he is of that number of whom it is said: *Rebuke a fool and he will go on to hate you* (Prv 9:8), then the disagreement is not born of love. But yet it does draw on and demonstrate the love of the reprover, because it is not hatred that is drawn out of him but that love which compelled him to rebuke and which endures unperturbed, even when the one who is reproved does hate. For if the one who corrects wants to return evil for evil to the one who is angered by correction, then he was not worthy to give that correction but clearly deserves correction himself.

Therefore behave in such a manner that indignation does not have a place among you, or if it has arisen let it be very quickly extinguished. Give more effort to making peace among yourselves than to arguing. For just as vinegar spoils a metal vessel if it stands in it too long ,[4] so anger spoils the heart if it is left overnight.[5] *Do these things, then, and the peace of God will be with you* (Phil 4: 9). At the same time pray for us, that we may eagerly put into practice the good advice which we have given to you.

Notes

1. The Latin original of Augustine's opening sentence, "*Bonus est dominus* et misericoridia eius est ubique diffusa, quae nos de vestra caritate in suis visceribus consolatur," would appear to be a play on Romans 5:5: *caritas dei diffusa est in cordibus nostris per Spiritum sanctum.*
2. See Mt 25:41.
3. See Ps 26(27):14; Is 25:9.
4. J. H. Baxter, *Saint Augustine: Select Letters* (Loeb ed.) 106, n. c, draws attention to the "vessel" metaphor in Horace, *Ep.* 1. 2. 54: *sincerum est nisi quodcumque infudis ascesit.* Augustine's classical education was not easily discarded.
5 . See Eph 4:26.

VI

The *Obiurgatio*

Augustine sends greetings in the Lord.

1. Just as severity is prepared to punish the sins that it finds, so charity does not want to find anything to punish. This was the reason why I did not come to you when you requested my very presence, since I would not have come to you to rejoice in your peace but to add to your dissensions. For how could have I treated lightly and left unpunished such a great uproar in my very presence as has assailed my ears in my absence, even though it did not meet my eyes? Perhaps, indeed, your rebellion would have been even greater in my presence, which [therefore] had to be denied you, since it would have been essential for your request not to be granted. It would have constituted a most deplorable precedent against good discipline, since what you sought was not in your own best interest, so that I *would find you not such as I would wish and be found myself not such as you would wish* (2 Cor 12:20).

2. Accordingly, since the apostle wrote to the Corinthians saying: *But I call God to witness upon my soul, it was to spare you that I have not yet come to you at Corinth, not because we lord it over your faith, but we are workers with you for your joy*, I also say to you: *It was to spare you that I did not come* (2 Cor 1:23). For I spared myself also, in case I should have *sorrow*

upon sorrow on your account (Phil 2:27; 2 Cor 2:3), and I chose not to show my face to you but *to pour out my heart* (Lam 2:19) to God for you and to deal with this very dangerous matter of yours not with words in your company but [alone] with God with tears, so that the joy with which I am accustomed to rejoice over you should not turn into grief, and to be a little comforted, among the great offences with which this world everywhere abounds, by thinking of your large congregation and chaste love, your holy way of living and the more abundant grace of God which has been given to you, so that you have not only scorned marriages of the flesh but, in addition, have chosen to be associated *in one mind in a house* (Ps 67:7 [68:6]), so that you may have *one soul and one heart* (Acts 4 :32) centered on God.

3. Reflecting upon these good gifts of God in you, among the many tempests by which it is shaken by other ills, my heart is accustomed, in some degree, to find rest. *You were running a good race* (Gal 5:7-9). *Who has bewitched you?* (Rom 3:1). *This persuasion is not from God, who called you. A little leaven . . .* (Gal 5: 8-9). I do not want to quote what follows, for I greatly desire, pray and exhort you that the *leaven* may turn to a better state, rather than that *the whole lump* may be turned—as it has almost turned—to a worse. If, then, you have blossomed afresh to a sound mind, *pray, that you may not enter into temptation* (Mt 26:41) and fall again into *quarrelings, envyings, anger, strifes, backbiting, tumults and whisperings* (2 Cor 12:20). For we did not so *plant* and *water* the Lord's garden among you so that we should *harvest thorns* from you (Jer 12:13; 1 Cor 3:6-8). If your weakness is still causing disorder, pray that you may be plucked from temptation. If, however, those who disturbed you still continue to do so, they shall bear the judgement, whoever they may be, unless they reform (Gal 5:10).

4. Consider what an evil it is, when we are rejoicing in the unity with the Donatists,[1] that we have to mourn internal divisions in a monastery! Persevere in your good purpose and you will not want to remove your superior. By having her in that outstanding monastery of yours for so many years, and by persevering there, you have grown in both numbers and maturity. She has been the mother not of your body but of your mind. All of you when you came to your monastery found her there, either serving and pleasing my late sister, the then superior,[2] or [later] being herself the superior who received you. Under her you were trained, under her you took the veil, under her you have increased in numbers, and now you are clamoring to have me remove her when you ought rather to grieve if I were to wish to do so. She is the one you know, the one to whom you came. For so many years, under her leadership, you have grown in numbers. You have received no new appointment, apart from the presbyter-in-charge, and if it is on his account that you seek something new and have rebelled against your mother in this way out of jealousy for him, why do you not rather ask for him to be changed? But if this latter suggestion appalls you—for I know how you love and revere him in Christ—why does not the former? For the attempts of the presbyter to govern you are cast into such disarray [by your disorder] that he would rather leave you than put up with these invidious accusations of yours, so that it is said that you would not have asked for another superior if you had not had him as presbyter? Let God therefore calm and compose your minds. Do not let *the work of the devil* (1 Jn 3:8) prevail among you, but let the peace of Christ *conquer in your hearts* (Col 3:15). Do not blush with shame and rush head-long into death by mental grief, embarrassed that what you wanted has not happened or because you are ashamed to

have wished what you ought not to have wished, but rather renew your salvation by being penitent. And it should not be the penitence of the traitor Judas[3] but rather the tears of the shepherd, Peter.[4]

Notes

1. CSEL text reads: *cum de deo natis. Cum donatistis* was a conjecture of the Benedictine editors, now confirmed by the Codex Turicensis (11th-12th centuries), the oldest complete text of the *Obiurgatio*. The Donatist Church, the great schismatic African communion, arose out of disputes over the validity of the orders conferred by bishops who had surrendered copies of the scriptures to the pagan authorities during the Diocletianic Persecution at the beginning of the fourth century and provoked some of Augustine's most important treatises on ecclesial and sacramental theology. In 411 at the Conference of Carthage, attended by bishops of the two rival Churches, the Roman imperial chairman, Count Marcellinus, himself a Catholic, decided that the *Catholica* was the legitimate Church of Africa and called for an end to the schism. This provides a *terminus post quem* for this letter. Subsequent imperial legislation ordered the compulsory reunion of the rival Churches.
2. See Possidius, *Life of Augustine* 26.1: "No woman ever frequented [Augustine's] house, no woman ever stayed there, not even his own sister, a widow consecrated to God, who ruled the maidservants of the Lord until her death." We have no other details of the sister's life.
3. See Mt 27:3-5.
4. See Mt 26:75.

VII

The *Regularis Informatio*

1.1 You that are settled in the monastery, these are the things that we advise you to observe.

1.2 In the first place—and this is the very reason for your being gathered together in one—you should live in the *house in unity of spirit* (Ps 67.7(68:6)) and you should have *one soul and one heart* centered on God (Acts 4:32).

1.3 And then, you should not call *anything your own, but you should have everything in common* (Acts 4:32). *Food and clothing* (1 Tm 6:8) should be allotted to you by your superior (*praeposita*), not equally to all because you are not all equally strong, but to each one according to need. For thus you read in the Acts of the Apostles: *They had everything in common and distribution was made to each as any had need* (Acts 4:32,35).

1.4 At the moment of entering the monastery those who had any property in the world should gladly choose to have it become common property.

1.5 As regards those who had no possessions, they should not seek to have in the monastery things which they could not have had outside. Yet if, because of illness, they are in need, they should be given whatever is

132

necessary, even though their poverty before entering was such that they could not even obtain necessities. They should not congratulate themselves on their good luck in finding the sort of food and clothing that they could not find outside.

1.6. Nor should they give themselves airs because they find themselves in the company of people whom they would not have dared to approach outside; but they should *lift their heart on high* and not be seeking *earthly things* (Col 3:1-2), which are transitory. Otherwise, monasteries will become profitable to the rich and not to the poor, if the rich become humble there and the poor become puffed up.

1.7 On the other hand, those who were regarded in the world as persons of consequence should not look down on their sisters who have entered the religious community from humble circumstances. They should take pains to glory in the companionship of their poor sisters rather than in the rank of wealthy relatives. They should not boast if they have contributed anything to the common life from their own means, nor should they take more pride in their riches because they are sharing them in the monastery than they would if they were enjoying them in the world. For every other vice prompts people to do evil deeds; but pride lies in ambush even for good deeds in order to destroy them. What advantage is it *to scatter abroad and give to the poor* (Ps 111 [112]: 9; 2 Cor 9:9) and become poor oneself, if the wretched soul becomes prouder in despising riches than it was in possessing them?

1.8   Therefore you should all live *united in mind and heart*
       (Acts 4:32) and should in one another honor God,[1]
       whose temples you have become.[2]

2.1   *Persevere faithfully in prayers* (Col 4:2) at the appointed
       hours and times.

2.2   In the oratory, no one should do anything that
       conflicts with its purpose, implied by its name. Hence
       if those who happen to be free wish to pray there
       outside the fixed hours they should not be hindered
       by anyone who might think of doing something else
       there.

2.3   When you pray to God in *psalms and hymns* (Col
       3:16), meditate in the heart on what is expressed with
       the voice.

2.4   And sing only what is set down for you to sing. But
       what is not written to be sung is not to be sung.

3.1   Discipline your flesh by fasting and abstinence from
       food and drink as far as your health allows. But when
       anyone cannot remain fasting, she should not take
       food apart from the midday meal unless she is ill.

3.2   When you come to table, and until you rise, you
       should listen without interruption or discussion to
       what is read to you according to custom. Not only do
       your throats take food[3] but ears, too, hunger *for the
       word of God* (Am 8:11).

3.3   If special treatment in the way of diet is given to those
       who are not strong as a result of their former way of
       life, others who are stronger because they have had a
       different manner of life must not be aggrieved or
       think it unfair. Nor should they think the former
       luckier in getting something that they themselves do

not get. Rather, they should be thankful that they are strong enough to do what others cannot.

3.4   When those who have entered the monastery from a more luxurious way of life are given any food, clothing, bedding or covering that is not given to others who are stronger and more fortunate, these latter should consider how far the former have come down from their previous way of life in the world, even though they cannot reach the simplicity of living which is possible for those who are stronger in body. All should not desire to receive the extra things which they see given to a few; such things are a concession, not an honor. Otherwise a detestable disorder would arise in the monastery if the rich work there as hard as ever they can, while the poor, who have greater strength, become soft.

3.5   As the sick need to eat little so that they do not become worse, so after illness they must certainly be given special care to help them to get strong as soon as possible, even if they came from conditions of extreme poverty in the world. In fact, recent illness has made necessary for them what a former way of life has made necessary for the rich. But when they have recovered their strength they should resume their own more fortunate way of life, since the less God's servants need the more fitting it is. The state of luxury by which their need was relieved when they were ill should not hold them there when they are better. They should esteem themselves to be the richer who are stronger in enduring privations. It is better to need less than to have more.

4.1 Your clothing should not be conspicuous. You should try to please not by your clothes but by your behavior. [Do not let your head-coverings be so thin that your hair-nets are visible under them, nor should you leave any part of your hair uncovered when outside the monastery, either carelessly hanging loose or elaborately arranged.]⁴

4.2 When you go out, walk together; and when you come to your destination, stay together.

4.3 In walking, in standing and in all your movements nothing should be done that might cause offence to anyone who sees you; everything should be in keeping with your holy state.

4.4 Even if your gaze chances to fall on a man you should not stare at him. There is no rule forbidding you to see men when you go out, but to attract or to encourage their attention is wrong.⁵ Nor is it only by touch and strong feelings that desire for men is aroused but also by the way of looking. You cannot claim to have pure minds if you have impure eyes, for an impure eye is the messenger of an impure heart. When impure hearts exchange messages by their glances, even though the tongue remains silent, and when through wrong desire they take pleasure in each other's ardor, then chastity takes flight from their behavior even though there has been no despoiling of the body.

4.5 Whoever lets her eye rest on a man and takes pleasure in having his rest on her should not imagine that she is not seen by others when she does so. She is bound to be noticed, and that by those she does not think have seen her. But even suppose she does conceal it and is seen by no human eye, what will she do about him who looks down from heaven and from whom nothing can be concealed?[6] Or are we to think that he does not see because his patience is as great as his wisdom? A woman consecrated to holiness, then, should fear to displease him[7], and then she will not want to please a man in a wrong way. She should ponder the fact that God sees all things, and then she will not want to look at a man in the wrong way. For it is fear of God that is commended to us in this connection, when it is written: *He who stares fixedly is an abomination to the Lord* (Prv 22:20 LXX).

4.6 Therefore when you are together in church or elsewhere where men are also present, you should protect one another's modesty, for in this way *God who dwells within you* (1 Cor 3:16; 1 Cor 6: 19; 2 Cor 6:16) will protect you from within yourselves.

4.7 And if you should notice in any one of you such wanton eyes as I am speaking of, you should warn her at once so that what has begun may go no further and may be immediately corrected.[8]

4.8 However, if after this warning you should see her do the same thing again, then or on another day, she who noticed it should report her as one who is hurt and in need of healing. First, however, it should be pointed out to a second or third person, so that she can be proved wrong by the *mouth of two or three witnesses* (Dt 19:15; Mt 18:16-17; 2 Cor 13:1) and can be restrained with whatever firmness seems suitable. Do not think that you are being a mischief-maker when you draw attention to this. On the contrary, you would be no more innocent yourselves if by silence you let your sisters be lost when by reporting the matter you could have corrected them. If your sister had a wound in her body which she wished to keep secret for fear of medical treatment, would it not be cruel to keep silent and compassionate to make it known? How much more, then, ought you to report her so that she does not suffer from a more terrible festering, that of the heart.

4.9   But before pointing it out to others by whom she could be proved in the wrong if she denies it, you should first report her to the superior, if after a warning she has still neglected to reform. This is in the hope that she may be corrected more privately without anyone else needing to know about it. But if she denies it, then without her knowledge others are to be brought in so that she may be accused and proved wrong not by one witness but *by two or three, in the presence of all* (Dt 19:15; Mt 18:16; 2 Cor 13:1; 1 Tm 5:20) . If indeed she is actually proved guilty she must accept such correction as will help her to amend, according to the judgement of the superior or of the presbyter, who has power to give direction and make judgements. If she refuses to accept this and yet does not withdraw of her own accord, she must be expelled from your fellowship.[9] And moreover this is not cruelty but compassion, lest she bring about the destruction of many by poisonous infection.

4.10   And what I have said about not staring unbecomingly is applied carefully and faithfully to the discovery, warning, reporting, proving and punishing in the field of other sins too, and that with love of the persons and hatred of the offenses.

4.11 Someone may have gone so far wrong as to receive letters or little gifts secretly from a man. Then, if she confesses of her own accord. she should be dealt with gently and prayer should be made for her. But if she should be found out and proved guilty she should be corrected more strictly at the discretion of the presbyter or the superior [or the other presbyters as a body or even by the bishop].

5.1 You should keep your clothes in one place under the care of one or two persons or as many as are needed to keep them shaken out and free from moths. Just as you are fed from a single storeroom, so you should be clothed from a single wardrobe. As far as possible, it should be a matter of indifference to you what is supplied for clothing according to the season—whether you receive what you left off or another garment which someone has had before—so long as no one is denied *what she needs* (cf. Acts 4:35). But if quarrels or murmurings arise among you on this account, and someone complains that she has received something that is not as good as what she had before, and she considers that it is beneath her dignity to wear what another sister has worn, this shows how far you are lacking in the holy interior clothing[10] of your heart, since you dispute about the clothing of the body. But even if concession is made to your weakness and you do receive what you left off, what you put aside must still be kept in one place under the common keepers.

5.2 So, then, no one should work at anything for herself [whether clothing or bedding or underwear or outer garments or a headdress]. All your work should be shared together with greater care and more ready eagerness than if you were doing things for yourself alone. For when it is written of *love* that it *does not seek its own* (1 Cor 13:5), it means that it puts the common good before its own and not personal advantage before the common good. Thus the more you are concerned about the common good rather than your own, the more progress you will know that you have made. And thus *the love that abides for ever* (1 Cor 13:13) will reign in all matters of passing necessity.

5.3 It follows that, should anyone bring anything to his or her daughters who are in the monastery, or to others with whom he or she has a particular link, whatever the gift—be it clothing or any other article that is considered a necessity—it should not be received secretly but be given to the superior for her to put into the *common stock* so that it may be offered *to anyone who needs it* (Acts 4:32.35). [If anyone conceals what is given to her, let her be condemned for theft.]¹¹

5.4 Your clothes are to be washed at the discretion of the superior, either by yourselves or by the fullers, so that too great a desire for clean clothing may not cause interior uncleanness of the mind. [Regarding the washing of the body or the use of the public baths, let it not be excessive, but let it be granted at the usual interval of time, namely once a month.]

5.5 Likewise, if someone's illness makes it necessary, bathing is not to be refused but on medical advice is to be done without murmuring. Even if a sister does not want it she must, at the command of the superior, do what has to be done for her health's sake. On the other hand, if she wants it and it is perhaps not expedient, she should not yield to her craving, for sometimes she thinks that what she likes will be good for her, when in fact it is harmful.

5.6 Finally, if one of the servants of God has a hidden pain and reports it, she is to be believed without hesitation; but if it is uncertain whether what she asks for can cure her pain the doctor should be consulted.

5.7 If you go to the baths, or wherever else it is necessary for you to go, there should not be fewer than three of you.[12] A sister who has to go out should not choose her own companions but should go with those whom the superior appoints.

5.8 The care of the sick—whether they are convalescent or suffering from any bodily weakness, even if there is no fever—should be entrusted to a particular person so that she may obtain from the storeroom what she sees each one needs.

5.9 Those who have charge of the storeroom, or the clothes, or the library, should serve their sisters without murmuring.

5.10 Books should be asked for at a definite time each day, and if anyone asks for them outside the time she should not be given them.

5.11 However, when there is need for clothes and shoes, those who have charge of them should not delay to give them as required.

6.1 Do not have quarrels, or at least bring them to an end as quickly as possible, lest anger grow into hatred—a straw into a plank—and produce a murderous heart.[13] [Nor do] the words: *Anyone who hates his brother is a murderer* (1 Jn 3:15) [apply only to men; for

the female sex has also received the precept, along
with the male which God has made first].

6.2   If anyone hurts another by abuse or cursing, or by
wild accusations, she should be careful to heal the
wound she has made by apologizing as soon as
possible; and the one who was hurt should herself be
careful to forgive without further discussion. But if
both have been hurtful they should forgive each
other's offence, remembering the prayers which,
because you repeat them so often, ought to be said
with complete sincerity. Nevertheless, it is better to
be one who is often tempted to give way to anger but
quick to ask forgiveness of the person she admits she
has injured than to be one who is more slowly roused
to anger but finds more difficulty in asking pardon.
Anyone who is never willing to ask pardon, or who
does not ask it from her heart, is in the monastery
without good reason, even if she is not expelled. You
should take care, then, not to use harsh words; but if
they have escaped from your mouth, then do not be
ashamed to let the mouth which caused the wound
provide the cure.

6.3   But if the necessity of good order compels you to
speak forcibly in order to put minors in their place,[14]
even if you yourself feel that you have gone too far, it
is not required of you to apologize to them. For it is
their duty to defer to you; and your power to act
should not be weakened by a display of excessive
humility. All the same, you should ask pardon of the
one who is Lord of all and who knows with what real
concern even those whom you may have reproved
more severely than is just are loved by you. Moreover,

even love among you must not be based on the standards of the world but on spiritual standards [for what immodest women do even to other women in jokes and other pranks ought not to be done at all not only by widows and virgins of Christ established in your holy profession but by any Christian women, whether married or marriageable].

7.1 You should obey your superior as you would a mother, with respect for her office, lest you offend God who is in her. This applies still more to the presbyter who has responsibility for you all.

7.2 It is chiefly the responsibility of the superior to see that all these instructions are complied with. If anything is not complied with, she should not let it lapse through negligence but should take care that the matter is corrected and put right; thus she will refer to the presbyter who has the greater authority among you anything that exceeds her own province or powers.

7.3 All the same, she should consider herself lucky not in having power over you but in being able to care for you with love (Gal 5:13; Rom 13:8-10).[15] Before you, she has to be at your head in honor; before God, she should be prostrate at your feet in fear. She should show herself to all around as a *model of good works* (Tit 2:7). She should *restrain the restless, encourage the faint-hearted, support the weak, be patient towards all* (1 Thes 5:14). She herself should keep these instructions gladly and so give them their due weight. And although both are necessary, she should seek rather your love than your fear, always bearing in mind the account she will have to render to God for you.

7.4   This is why, by being the more obedient, you show compassion not only to yourselves but also to her, for the higher the position held among you the greater the peril her who holds it.

8.1   May the Lord grant that you observe all these things with love, as lovers of *spiritual beauty,*[15] radiating by your good life the *sweet odor of Christ* (2 Cor 2:15), not like *slaves under the law but as free persons established in grace* (Rom 6:14).

8.2   And so that you may be able to look at yourselves in this little book *as in a mirror,*[16] it should be read to you once a week, lest you neglect anything through forgetfulness. When you find that you are doing the things that are written give thanks to the Lord, the giver of all good things. But when any one of you sees that she has failed in some way, she should be sorry for the past and be on her guard for the future, praying that her *sin may be forgiven* and that she may not be *led into temptation* (Mt 6:12-13; Lk 11:4).

Notes

1. See Rom 15:5-6.
2. See 2 Cor 6:16.
3. See Mt 4:4.
4. Passages in brackets do not appear in the *Praeceptum*. The reference to hair-nets *(retiola)* also occurs in Augustine's *Holy Virginity 34*: "Nor am I concerned with those who seek to please, either with dress more elegant than the needs of their high calling demand, or with a bandeau conspicuous whether with protruding knots of hair or with veils so thin that the hair-nets lying below become visible *(ut retiola subter posita appareant)*" (trans. By P. G. Walsh, *Augustine, De bono coniugali. De sancta virginitate* (Oxford: Clarendon Press, 2001) 112. The treatise is probably to be dated to 401, though M. F. Berrouard suggests c. 397.
5. See Mt 5:28.
6. See Prv 24:12.
7. See Prv 24:18.
8. See Mt 18:15.
9. See Mt 18:17.
10. See Ti 2:3. *In habitu sancto.* Some English versions have "reverent in behavior."
11. This sentence has found its way into the *Regula Recepta*.
12. The *Praeceptum* has "two or three."
13. See Mt 7:3-5.
14. See above, p. 107, note 13.
15. Sir 44:6 Vulgate: *pulchritudinis studium habentes.*
16. See Jas 1:23-25.

Bibliography

Critical Editions of Texts

Praeceptum: Verheijen, *Règle* I, 417-437; reprinted in Lawless, *Augustine of Hippo and his Monastic Rule*, 80-109.

Ordo Monasterii: Verheijen, I, 148-52 (with misprint *mena* for *mense,* p. 149, line 12); reprinted in Lawless, 74-79.

Obiurgatio: Verheijen, I, 49-53; reprinted in Lawless, 104-109.

Regularis Informatio: Verheijen, I, 53-66; Lawless gives only a translation.

Praeceptum Longius: edd. F. Villegas & A. de Vogüé, *CSEL* 87,3-16 ; reprinted in Maximilian Krausgruber, *Die Regel des Eugippius. Die Klosterordnung des Verfassers der Vita Severini im Lichte ihrer Quellen.* Text, Übersetzung und Kommentar. (Frühes Christentum. Forschungen und Perspektiven Bd. 2) (Thaur bei Innsbruck:: Kulturverlag, 1996), 72-93.

Regula Recepta: Constitutiones Ordinis Fratrum S. Augustini (Rome 1968); ed. and trans. by Robert P. Russell, O.S.A., *The Rule of our Holy Father Augustine* (Villanova University Press, 1992).

Epistula Longior = Augustine, *Letter* 211. *CSEL* 57, 359-371.

Epistula Longissima: ed. A. C. Vega, *Miscellenea Giovanni Mercati* 2 (Studi e Testi 122) (Rome 1946) 47-56; reprinted in *PL Suppl.* 2, 349-356.

The Rule of the Master: Latin text: *Sources chrétiennes* 105 and 106 (Paris 1966); E.T. by Luke Eberle; introduction by Adalbert de Vogué, trans. by Charles Philippi (Kalamazoo, MI: Cistercian Publications, 1977).

The Rule of St. Benedict: Sources chrétiennes 181-186 (Paris 1971-1972); Trans.: *RB 1980: The Rule of St. Benedict. In Latin and English*, with notes, ed. by Timothy Fry, OSB, (Collegeville, Mich., 1991).

Selected Modern Studies

Agatha Mary, S.P.B., *The Rule of Saint Augustine. An Essay in Understanding* (Villanova, Penn.: Augustinian Press, 1992).

Arbesman, Rudolf, "The Question of the *Regula Sancti Augustini," Augustinian Studies* 1 (1970) 237-261.

Hand, Thomas A., *Augustine on Prayer*, new ed. (New York: Catholic Book Publishing Co., 1986).

Hoare, F. R., *The Western Fathers* (London / New York: Sheed and Ward Ltd., 1954).

Lambot, C., "Saint Augustin a-t-il rédigé la règle pour moines qui porte son nom?" *Revue Bénédictine* 53 (1941) 41-58.

Lawless, George P., "The Rule of Saint Augustine as a Mirror of Perfection," *Angelicum* 58 (1981) 460-474.

_____. "Enduring Values of the Rule of Augustine," *Angelicum* 59 (1982) 59-78.

_____. "Ordo Monasterii: Structure, Style and Rhetoric," *Augustinianum* 59 (1982) 469-491.

_____. "Psalm 132 and Augustine's Monastic Ideal," *Angelicum* 59 (1982) 526-539.

_____. *Augustine of Hippo and his Monastic Rule* (Oxford: The Clarendon Press, 1987; paperback edition).

Mandonnet, Pierre, *Saint Dominique*, 2 vols. (Paris, 1937).

Taft, Robert F., *The Liturgy of the Hours in East and West. The Origins of the Divine Office and Its Meaning For Today* (Collegeville, Minn.: Liturgical Press, 1986) 94-96.

van Bavel, Tarcisius. *The Rule of Saint Augustine. Masculine and Feminine Versions*. Trans. by Raymond Canning (London: Darton, Longman and Todd, 1983).

Verheijen, Luc, "Remarques sur le style de la 'Regula Secunda' de Saint Augustin," *Augustinus Magister* (Paris: Etudes Augustiniennes, 1954) I, 255-63.

_____. *La Règle de Saint Augustin*. 2 vols. (Paris: Études Augustiniennes, 1967).

_____. *Saint Augustine's Monasticism in the Light of Acts 4. 32-35* (The Saint Augustine Lecture 1975) (Villanova University Press, 1979).

_____. *Nouvelle approche de la Régle de Saint Augustin* (Vie monastique 8) (Bégrolles en Mauges, 1980).

Zumkeller, Adolar, *Augustine's Ideal of the Religious Life*. Trans. by Edmund Colledge (New York: Fordham University Press, 1986).

_____. *Augustine's Rule. A Commentary*. Trans. by M. J. O'Connell (Villanova, Penn.: Augustinian Press, 1987).